Is China Unstable?

Published in cooperation with the Sigur Center
for Asian Studies, George Washington University.

Studies on Contemporary China

Is China Unstable?

Assessing the Factors

David Shambaugh
Editor

Thomas P. Bernstein
Pieter Bottelier
Bruce J. Dickson
June Teufel Dreyer
Merle Goldman
Steven F. Jackson
Nicholas R. Lardy
H. Lyman Miller
Dorothy J. Solinger
Martin King Whyte

An East Gate Book

M.E. Sharpe
Armonk, New York
London, England

An East Gate Book

Library of Congress Cataloging-in-Publication Data

Is China unstable? : assessing the factors / David Shambaugh, editor
p. c.m.—(Studies on contemporary China)
Includes bibliographical references and index.
ISBN 0-7656-0572-4 (cloth : alk. paper). — ISBN 0-7656-0573-2 (pbk. : alk. paper)
1. China—Economic conditions—1976– 2. Economic stabilization—China. 3.
China—Politics and government—1976– I. Shambaugh, David L. II. Series.

HC427.92.I8 2000
306'.0951'09049—dc21 99-050215
CIP

Printed in the United States of America

The paper used in this publication meets the minimum requirements of
American National Standard for Information Sciences
Permanence of Paper for Printed Library Materials,
ANSI Z 39.48-1984.

∞

BM (c) 10 9 8 7 6 5 4 3 2 1
BM (p) 10 9 8 7 6 5 4 3 2 1

Dedicated to the memory of Seiki Katsuo

Contents

Preface

There is probably no more pertinent question for all who deal with China today than that of China's potential for instability. This is true not only for analysts, but also nations, investors, and traders who have large-scale commitments in the country. If China becomes unstable, it will have significant global implications.

The question of China's instability is, of course, a perennial one, given China's convulsive history of domestic rebellions, territorial fragmentation, warlords, poverty, famine, disease, war, and revolution. In the fifty years of the People's Republic of China, the country has experienced repeated instances of instability—many induced by the Maoist regime and the Chairman himself. Indeed, over the millennia, it is probably fair to say that China has known more instability than stability. Instability can come in a number of sectors—economically, socially, politically—and it can arise seemingly suddenly. Like an earthquake, analysts may be able to identify early-warning indicators, but can never predict precisely how and when they will coalesce and erupt.

In an attempt to assess the existing factors that could give rise to instability in China today, The Sigur Center for Asian Studies at George Washington University convened a conference on June 19, 1998. In this effort, the contributors to this volume were joined by leading China specialists from the U.S. government and intelligence community, Washington-area universities and research institutes, foreign embassies, and journalists with extensive experience in China. The conference considered earlier drafts of the revised papers contained in this volume,[1] and engaged in a thorough discussion of the factors contributing to both stability and instability in China today. Neither the conference nor this volume proceeded from a supposition that China *was* unstable—it merely asked the question, defined the potential parameters of instability, and assessed the relevant factors that may give rise to an unstable China.

The contributions to this volume clearly indicate that, at the turn of the millenium, China possesses a large number of unstable factors and elements. But they also point to a number of stabilizing variables, and generally concluded with one participant that, while volatile and becoming more so in the wake of the Asian financial crisis, China today is in a curiously ambivalent state of "stable unrest" that may continue for some time. Numerous "nodes" of instability exist throughout the society, but with little apparent connecting tissue to create a critical mass. At the same time, it was agreed that China today is more unstable than at any time since the height of the Cultural Revolution (1966–1969). Moreover, many of the factors that challenged the Communist party-states in the former Soviet Union and Eastern Europe and contributed to their gradual demise and ultimate overthrow are present in China today. But so too are key factors not previously present in these other countries—notably a growing economy, extensive trade and investment ties to the outside world, a generally cohesive multiethnic society, a stable political leadership, and strong regime control over the military and internal security services. On balance, these factors were judged to be predominant at present and would buffer the party-state from challenges from below or within. Nonetheless, the contributors to this volume and participants in the conference all agreed that the factors and forces of potential instability in China today are strong and growing, and that no reasonable analyst would be wise to assume indefinite socio-political-economic stability, or continuance of Communist Party rule, in China.

This project owes its origins to discussions I had with several Japanese colleagues—notably Professors Kokubun Ryosei and Kojima Tomoyuki of Keio University in Tokyo. Unfortunately, due to last-minute difficulties, neither was able to participate in the conference or contribute to the volume, but their intellectual input was significant. I am also most grateful for financial support from the Japan External Trade Research Organization (JETRO) and its affiliated Global Industries and Social Progress Research Institute (GISPRI). The Institute's dynamic late executive director Seiki Katsuo was also instrumental in supporting and shaping this project from the beginning, and it is a great pity he did not live to see its fruition. The volume is accordingly dedicated to his memory. I also wish to thank Dorothy Solinger and Thomas Bernstein for continually urging me to submit this for publication as a book, so that it would have a longer "shelf life" and circulate more widely than the earlier version, which was published as a research report.[2] Finally, thanks are due to Doug Merwin, Asian Studies editor *extraordinaire* at M.E. Sharpe, for recognizing the potential interest in this volume and publishing it.

David Shambaugh

Washington, D.C.

Notes

1. The chapters herein have not been substantially revised since the summer of 1998.

2. David Shambaugh (ed.), *Is China Unstable? Assessing the Factors* (Washington, D.C.: Sigur Center for Asian Studies, *Asia Paper* No. 2, 1998).

Is China Unstable?

1
Introduction: A Typology for Stability and Instability in China

Steven F. Jackson

"I have stated our position that with regard to the political disturbances in 1989, had the Chinese Government not taken the resolute measures, then we could not have enjoyed the stability that we are enjoying today."

—*Jiang Zemin*

President Jiang's statement during his televised debate in Beijing with President Clinton may be the "bottom-line" rationalization of the Chinese leadership for the Tiananmen Square massacre, but it begs an even more important question today: *Is China unstable?* The question may not be easy to answer, but it is vital for the interests of America, Asia, and the world. Consider for a moment what is at stake in China's stability:

- The lives and welfare of more than 1.3 billion people;
- The world's fastest growing economy over the past two decades, the second largest recepient of foreign direct investment, and possessing the world's second largest cache of foreign exchange reserves;
- One of the world's largest trading economies, with total annual trade exceeding $300 billion including $90 billion in U.S.–China trade;

- A nuclear power, with missiles capable of striking the continental United States, and an increasingly powerful conventional military power;
- A nation bordering fourteen countries, many of them with their own problems of stability, and a permanent seat on the UN Security Council.

The stakes are extraordinarily high, and there is ample evidence to warrant careful consideration of the issue and its potential. Consider, for example, the impact on Asia of a large-scale refugee exodus from China—stimulated by social or political instability.

The financial crisis of East and Southeast Asian economies that started in Thailand and then spread to Indonesia, South Korea, and elsewhere has led to a crisis of confidence in Hong Kong and has affected China. There is evidence that China's economy is faltering. China has more unemployed workers today—as many as 150 million in all categories—than most countries have people. The reform of state-owned enterprises (SOEs) has imperiled the jobs of millions more who work in inefficient factories dating from the Stalinist era, particularly in the interior and Northeast regions of China. Rural discontentment has also manifested itself in a variety of forms, ranging from protests and petitions to riots, some involving thousands of people. Burdened by arbitrary and often unfair taxes and levies, Chinese farmers have shown a willingness to resort to extreme means to gain attention and redress. In areas populated by ethnic minorities, the central authority of Beijing must be exerted by force—often brutally. As Martin King Whyte's contribution reminds us, these and other sources of instability are increasingly straining the state, as channels to vent popular grievance are far from sufficient.

Within the ruling Chinese Communist Party (CCP), the loss of any sort of Marxist ideological drive and the booming economy has resulted in opportunities for self-enrichment for one's self and family. This corruption has become an endemic and corrosive drain on the system. There is substantial evidence that the top leadership of China constantly worries about the stability of their country and sustenance of their rule. Perhaps indicative of this insecurity was the recent formation of a high-level Leading Group for Comprehensive Public Order. Examples such as the collapse of the USSR and the downfall of President Suharto of Indonesia serve as constant reminders that the apparently firm hold of a ruling party or leader may indeed be very fragile.

All of this evidences a plain fact: China is facing enormous problems. But, as H. Lyman Miller's chapter reminds us, this characterization has been true for the past 150 years. The question is whether these enormous problems threaten the fundamental stability of the world's most populous country?

It is worth remembering that for any country in the late twentieth century, too much stability can be deleterious, too; the Brezhnevian Soviet Union was stable, to be sure, but at enormous long-term costs. Stability and instability are merely points along a continuum of change and dynamism. The question becomes one of how much change and what kinds of popular reaction to change exist? The appended matrix is an attempt to summarize the stability continuum, from hyperstability to complete collapse a la Yugoslavia or the former USSR. The vertical axis indicates the social segment, starting from the most powerful at the top (elite), and working downward toward the least powerful segments, farmers and minorities, much like the order in which the conference papers were presented. For each cell in the matrix, conditions and political actions are described. The relationship of the cells is not completely independent, particularly the relationship of the higher cells to the lower cells.

Leadership Stability, Army Loyalty, Party Corruption

Despite the considerable evidence of substantial pockets of instability in places and segments of China, David Shambaugh's contribution suggests that there is little evidence of leadership or military instability as far as can be known. President Jiang Zemin appears to have a firm leadership position, and the factionalism that characterized past decades of Chinese leadership is not in evidence. The triumvirate of President and Party leader Jiang Zemin, National People's Congress (NPC) head Li Peng, and Premier Zhu Rongji achieved not only a remarkably smooth transition of power after the death of paramount leader Deng Xiaoping, but also a solidification of their power at the 15th Party Congress. Rival leaders such as Qiao Shi and others are now demoted into comfortable retirement, and the last echoes of even mildly leftist thinking in party elder Deng Liqun is being marginalized. Economic Czar Zhu Rongji's position, however, is neither clear nor consolidated. Although some believe that Zhu has managed to promote a few key members of his group into second and third-tier advisory positions, others think that Zhu has risen beyond his base of support. In any case, Zhu's emphasis and association with economic policy does make him politically vulnerable—some might say expendable—should the economy have serious problems such as dropping significantly below the target figure of 8 percent annual growth (this figure has often been cited by the leadership as the desired necessary rate for national growth, above which inflation becomes likely and below which there may not be enough opportunity to keep citizens happy or at least quiet).

Beneath the top leadership lies the military, whose leaders have been undergoing a rapid overhaul and professionalization in recent years. With one or two exceptions—Chi Haotian being one—the new army commanders are characterized as former unit commanders, not the commissars or personnel of the General Political Department (GPD) of the People's Liberation Army (PLA, which also includes the navy and airforces). These officers tend to be highly professional but hardly cosmopolitan, and have little foreign travel outside of the invasions of Vietnam (1979), India (1962), and Korea (1950). There is no reason to question their loyalty to the regime at the present time. The regime also has at its disposal another large coercive instrument in the People's Armed Police, a paramilitary force which not only has riot control equipment, but also is composed of "demobilized" army units with heavy equipment.

Impressive though the coercive instruments of the top leaders may be, Bruce Dickson's contribution shows that Chinese Communist Party cadres and rank and file are in much worse shape to direct the country. The traditional membership base of the CCP, the workers and peasants, form considerably less of the party's membership today, and are being replaced by more educated urban elements. The one group that has been fairly successfully recruited into the Communist Party has been, ironically, businessmen and women. Party recruitment at lower levels in the fastest growing parts of the Chinese economy, the non-state sector, however, has been disappointing; highly mobile non-state sector workers simply do not bother joining the party. Recruitment among the "floating population" is almost impossible, nor is it desireable. The result is that other forms of authority are forming: managers on the workshop floor, in villages the leaders of clans and in some areas religious groups. The reaction of local party officials to these new groups has not been simple or consistent, sometimes violently opposing them, sometimes cooperating or attempting to co-opt them.

The Critical Context: The Economy

There is little doubt that the economy is the key to Chinese stability; the core question is how good or bad the economy really is, and whether it can withstand the short-term shocks of State Owned Enterprise (SOE) reform in the transition to an almost wholly market-based economy. Nicholas Lardy's contribution shows that the reasons for pessimism are primarily financial: China has little ability to moderate and finely control its macroeconomic fluctuations through monetary levers. This has led in the past to only two speeds for the Chinese economy: full-speed to the point of overheating, and all-stop (though some participants pointed out that the Chinese economy has shown a greater ability to "land softly" in the 1990s than before). A slowdown could lead to significant pressure on the banking system, because many Chinese enterprises are highly indebted to banks, and up to 25 percent of these loans are—by Western accounting methods—non-performing. The situation of bad debt is not helped by the low real interest rates charged by Chinese banks, which has led to a flood of credit to uncreditworthy firms. Many Chinese firms own six times more debt than equity, a ratio worse than South Korean chaebol before the economic crisis of the summer of 1997. As summarized by Nicholas Lardy, ". . . loans outstanding from all financial institutions in China increased almost 40 fold, from RMB 190 billion at year-end 1978 to RMB 7.5 trillion at year-end 1997. Relative to the size of the economy loans doubled over this period and by year-end 1997 were fully equal to gross domestic product." The key to the situation is SOE reform, which will help stop the conversion of good loans into bad debt, though this has its own risks:

> . . . pushing through fundamental reform of state-owned enterprises is fraught with risks. Rising unemployment, even if it is only transitory, could precipitate massive labor unrest, which could easily derail the real sector restructuring that is so badly needed. Delaying or slowing the current reforms in the short run might mitigate some of the adverse social and political consequences of reform. But its long term consequence would be the loss of the opportunity to create a more efficient system of resource allocation and utilization. Thus delay almost certainly would eventually cause an even lower pace of economic growth, an even slower pace of job creation, and ultimately an even greater challenge to political stability. Thus the leadership may have little alternative but to push its current reform agenda aggressively.

The aggressive approach to SOE reform associated with Zhu Rongji has so far continued, but it is likely to have serious consequences in those industrial areas of China which are less export-oriented and competitive, such as the Northeast and the interior. Even relatively efficient Shanghai could see a large number of firms closed.

These problems, however, do not necessarily mean that China is on the verge of economic collapse—far from it. As Pieter Bottelier demonstrates, China possesses some substantial economic advantages. First and foremost, China is not directly vulnerable to the Asian financial crisis in the ways that other countries in the region have been. China's massive foreign exchange reserves of $144 billion, minimal short-term debt exposure, and its current account surplus provides the ability to ride out short-term trade deficits. China also does not have a freely convertible currency for capital account transfers or a large amount of short-term debt as did South Korea, and thus the *Renminbi* (RMB) is not vulnerable to monetary speculation in the ways that the rupiah, won, baht, yen, and other currencies have been in the last year. In fact, the RMB has appreciated against the U.S. dollar, the only Asian currency to do so. In short, Bottelier concludes, "...the probability of instability in China due to external economic pressures or macroeconomic imbalances remains low." Second, China continues to have a high rate of GDP growth, though it has slowed in recent years. The key question is whether the government can maintain a rate of growth around 8 percent. Third, rural discontentment notwithstanding (see below), harvests in China have been good for the past three years and grain stocks are at an all-time high, a relief for any nation which must feed 1.3 billion people. Externally, China has great strengths, but internally it must solve its financial problem before it becomes a crisis.

Intellectual Quiescence, Dissidents in Exile

Merle Goldman's contribution is a reminder that students and intellectuals who had formed the vanguard of the 1989 democracy movement are now largely alienated or apolitical in China. The main targets of recent government control has been those activists who were involved in previous protest movements, such as Wei Jingshen and Wang Dan, both arrested and exiled. Wei and Wang, however, have very different perspectives on events in China, and whereas Wang has made extensive contacts in the Chinese exile community, Wei is much more of a loner, and years of imprisonment have left him somewhat out of touch with current conditions in China. Chinese authorities have clamped down especially hard on those activists who have attempted to link up different and isolated groups such as labor activists. Government control over dissidents is made more complicated these days by the growth of the "virtual democracy wall" in China and the rapid growth of the World Wide Web. It is not surprising, therefore, that Chinese police often confiscate dissidents' computers when they arrest them.

On a different side of the political spectrum, the remnants of the leftists who question the pace and scope of reform in China are in an increasingly marginalized position in China as well. Led by party elder Deng Liqun, this group has been somewhat critical of the rapid pace of economic reforms. The Communist Party subsidies to their activities are likely to end soon, leaving them without a major mouthpiece or institutional home.

China today faces a difficult situation; on the one hand, experiments with village-level elections are occurring, and there has been a very impressive opening of the atmosphere of discussion and discourse during the past year. Although many conference participants disagreed with the characterization, others felt that the current political climate in China is one of the most open since 1979, something the American media has failed to adequately report. The possibilities of political reform are again being discussed in the scholarly journals in China, such as Li Shenzhi's 1998 article in *Gaige* and other journals. On the other hand, it is clear that no reappraisal of the June 4, 1989 "incident" is imminent, dissidents are still closely monitored (particularly if they try to make connections with other dissidents or labor leaders), and the extent to which village level democracy will be allowed to "trickle up" the system has not yet been determined.

Worker Games, State Losses

Urban unrest and, in particular, labor actions form another area of potential instability in China. This is the subject of Dorothy Solinger's chapter. Given the large number of unemployed workers and soon-to-be unemployed workers if SOE reform is pushed vigorously, one might expect to see organized strikes, wildcat strikes, sit-downs, protests, and other worker actions. These are occurring in China, have been occurring for more than a decade now, but are accelerating in scale and scope.

Furthermore, both management and workers have developed arsenals of tactics for gaining what they want from the other. Workers want to keep their jobs, and management (and directly or indirectly the state) wants them to keep working and the situation to remain stable. But in a rapidly changing economic environment, workers are often implicitly or explicitly threatened and respond. Sometimes the response is harassment, demonstrations, petitions, letters to higher government levels, protests, slowdowns, and even strikes and plant vandalism.

The state has its own arsenal, too, and it not only consists of the coercive "sticks" of police, and the heavily-armed People's Armed Police; the state also possesses "carrots": bailing out factories and firms which cannot make their payrolls. The cost of such bailouts, however, is likely to mount as SOE reform proceeds, and runs directly opposite the fiscal policy of Zhu Rongji. As reform proceeds, this tension is likely to be seen more frequently, though to different degrees in different areas: higher in the industrial Northeast and interior, and less along the coast and South. What remains unclear is the degree to which worker resentment will be directed against their factory managers, local party leaders, or against the pinnacle of the system: the top leadership and the Communist Party.

The reaction of workers to recent SOE reform efforts is still tentative and it is probably too soon to tell how they will react to large-scale layoffs. The research that has been done on the issue would indicate, however, that workers retain a faith in the commitment of the state to provide the most basic of welfare assurances (food at a minimum) and a pessimism in their own ability to do much more than protest. Workers at foreign-owned firms in coastal regions are too disorganized to mount more than short-lived labor actions. Although the Communist Party no longer has control of the shop floor in the "neo-traditionalist" manner of divide and conquer in the way it once did, managers now assume the role of state representatives. The organizational capabilities of the state, to move either coercive or remunerative instruments around the country to deal with piece-meal strikes and instability would make it appear that worker unrest is not likely to turn into major urban instability in the short run.

Rural Discontentment, Nascent Democracy?

Thomas Bernstein's contribution on the rural sector tells us that peasants are unhappy in much of China today, and frequently with good reason: informal taxation, fees, fines, appropriations, and other revenue extractions by local officials place burdens on farmers range from the irritating to the ruinous. Government payments for agricultural products in IOUs instead of cash led to similar discontentment in 1992–93, and land requisitioning and pollution are major problems in areas in which rural industry is growing. Added to this are the frequent resentment of peasants against the government for its birth control policies, corruption of local officials, and their often gross abuse of power.

Resentment has led to confrontations, many of which have been violent. For example, the 1993 riots in Renshou County, Sichuan, where between 10,000 and 15,000 peasants were involved. According to one report, there were over 6,000 incidents in rural China in 1993, with a total of over 8,000 casualties. Protests, demonstrations, and petitions to the government have also occurred.

Isolated incidents of confrontations and violence, however, do not necessarily lead to national-level instability. First of all, these incidents tend to be regionally concentrated in the poorer interior provinces such as Hunan, Hubei, Anhui, and Jiangxi. The areas most likely to be affected by rural unrest are those places where it has occurred in previous years. In some cases, the history of unrest in these particular localities goes back years, decades, or even centuries. The coastal areas have experienced unrest, but for different reasons (e.g., land appropriation and pollution), and with less intensity. Second, rural confrontations have tended to be short-lived, local, and spontaneous, a problem that is briefly intense but not sustained. Occasionally peasant unrest and violence does begin to exhibit a degree of organization and leadership, often supplied by local party cadres directed against their superiors. Sustained organizations that span more than a few townships in a county, however, are quite rare. Most of the actions are grievances, meant to force local officials to adhere to laws and regulations, and are not politically motivated. But in many cases, peasants currently have no clear and direct means to redress their grievances, and suffer grievously when local officials arrive with security forces to "shake down" a village for more revenue.

The one positive aspect of rural China that would seem to have the potential for counterbalancing the discontentment there is the growing use of village elections to select leaders and representatives to basic decision-making bodies. Specifically in the case of the Renshou riots, these failed to spread to a neighboring county where officials had been locally elected. The growing interest in village-level elections in China should be tempered somewhat with the realization that the implementation of these elections varies widely across China. Nor does there seem to be any particular pattern of electoral practice:

> Despite the large number of case studies of local elections, there seems to be no relationship between meaningful elections and such things as local standards of living, rate of growth, level of literacy, etc. What matters most is not these standard measures of modernization, but instead the attitude of local party and government leaders, which is hard to predict. Elections have been most successful where township and county leaders are supportive of elections and increased political participation (Dickson).

In no cases do the candidates challenge the basic political structure of China, the dominance of the Communist Party, or other fundamentals. Within these constraints, however, there are competitive candidates, who make electoral promises which might be familiar to American voters: more jobs, fairer taxes, better implementation of central policies. Party membership is not required for candidacy in these elections, but the representatives who are elected are often then recruited into the CCP.

Minority Unrest

The one area in which there is clearly a substantial degree of instability in China is the minority regions, and in particular Tibet, Xinjiang, and Inner Mongolia, which border hostile India, Mongolia, Kazakhstan, and the unstable Kyrgyz Republic which have ethnic compatriots just across the border. June Teufel Dreyer's contribution explains how a combination of domestic and foreign factors have increased instability in minority areas, and the response of the central government has been two pronged: firm, often brutal suppression of ethnic uprisings, and an effort to promote economic growth in minority areas. Neither strategy has succeeded in quelling the problems.

Economic reform has not had a uniformly positive impact in all areas of China; the interior areas have not done as well as coastal areas, and minority areas which are almost all interior have done quite poorly. The income gap between the dominant Han Chinese and minorities has grown, and economic progress in minority areas has created resentment between Han and non-Han and within minorities themselves.

Exacerbating these difficulties has been a more complex international environment. Islamic fundamentalism has brought a new influence to the Muslim areas of Xinjiang, and nationalist governments in Mongolia, Turkey, Kazakhstan, and the former Soviet Union have added to ethnic identity and appeal. Even for those ethnic areas which have prospered with economic reform, the result has not necessarily been gratitude toward the government in Beijing or an increase in identity with China; leisure has sometimes led to greater ethnic identity with kin across international boundaries, and the activities of "journalists" and activists from outside China has led the Chinese state to crack down harshly against ethnic unrest. This in turn has led to Western criticism particularly of the Chinese occupation of Tibet, Chinese defensiveness and reaction, and further unrest. There is some evidence of connection between ethnic dissidents in Tibet and Mongolia, based upon their common lamistic Buddhist heritage, but connections to Han dissidents and other ethnic groups are few.

Outlook

China is facing some enormous problems with pockets of unrest, discontentment, protest, and in a few isolated cases, outright rebellion do exist. But does that mean that China is *unstable*? We must return to the difficult issue of defining *stability* and *instability*. If we define stability or instability as points along a continuum, between stagnation and rapid regime collapse similar to the Soviet Union or Yugoslavia, then China on balance lies somewhere in the middle, toward the "disruption" side. Referring again to the stability typology matrix, China would appear to have different segments which exhibit different tendencies. Note that movement along the horizontal axis of the matrix implies increasing frequency, intensity, and areas of occurrence of actions. The vertical axis indicates political power, or lack thereof. If any generalization about China today can be made, it would be that as one moves down the table in the segments, there is more evidence for instability than at the top of the segments; elites show little evidence of instability, whereas minorities show the greatest instability, followed by the rural sectors. This is substantially different than the profile of China on the eve of the Cultural Revolution, where elite instability was high and rural instability was low. Thus, historically, movement toward the right on the higher cells has far greater effect than similar movement within the lower cells. Higher cells such as elites, military, and students have an ability to "drag" the lower cells with them, but the lower cells' ability to drag upper cells limited. The indecision of the elites in how to respond to the Tiananmen protests in the spring of 1989, coupled with the students' movement linking up with workers led to a serious crisis in 1989.

It is this linkage between segments and between geographical areas that becomes critical to the larger stability of China. Chinese dynasties endured rebellions for decades without falling so long as those rebellions were disconnected, uncoordinated, and geographically dispersed. The current state of China is such that disruption in parts of the interior such as Sichuan and the minority areas is greatest, but the connection between minorities and ethnic Chinese rural discontentment is non-existent. Peasant unrest is substantial, but mostly localized and sporadic, and occurs more often in the interior provinces than along the coast. Worker unrest exists, but it too is regionally centered, focused upon factory issues, and dealt with fairly easily given the resources of the state. Student leadership and example, which often provides the key connection between elite issues and popular discontentment such as seen in Indonesia, appears to be largely absent in China today. It is little wonder that the state in the last few years has reacted most harshly against those dissidents and activists who have sought to make connections with other dissidents in different parts and segments of China; that would represent the linkage that could possibly destabilize the country.

One must conclude with substantial caution: those who attempt to predict the future of China are all too often proven wrong. China in 1945 appeared stable; World War II was won, the KMT under Chiang Kai-shek was firmly in control, with only a tiny communist dissident element in far-away Yan'an; four years later, those same communists under Mao Zedong had taken over the country and turned China upside down. China in 1965 also appeared to be stable; within two years the country was in the turmoil of the Cultural Revolution. China in 1988 would have appeared to be fairly stable and prosperous, only to undergo the convulsions of protests, economic retrenchment, and Tiananmen Square massacre and subsequent crackdown. Any prediction of stability in China must of necessity be a relative one and a contingent one. Much rides on the success of continued economic reform, and in particular reform of the SOEs. Much rides on dealing with the enormous financial problem before it can turn into a crisis. Much depends on allowing greater participation in decision making, room for open discourse, and open methods of dealing with corruption and malfeasance.

Appendix

Stability Typology

Hyperstability

Condition / Segment	*Stagnation*	*Stasis*	*Dynamic equilibrium*
elite	no elite turnover	elite turnover is slow, no attempts at systemic changes	periodic turnover by systemic means resulting in incremental policy changes
military	aristocratic or non-meritocratic promotion	little turnover or promotion; doctrinal stagnation	regular turnover and professional training
students/ intellectuals	no intellectual development; rote memorization of orthodoxy	pre-professional, tracked system with little diversity or involvement in politics	some political interest and diversity of opinion
workers	immobility, inherited trades, guild domination	low turnover, low mobility	high sectoral and geographic labor mobility; labor organization is sectorally differentiated
unemployed	persistent and wide-spread, marginalized	low visible unemployment due to relatively closed labor market	high frictional unemployment and movements between areas and sectors in search of jobs
farmers	pervasive landlord-tenant relations, no improvements in productivity, peasants bound formally or informally to land	independent yeoman farmers, low mobility but independence	complex urban-rural migration; establishment of non-agricultural rural economy; trade and commercialization of agriculture
minorities	subordination, lack of involvement	forced integration or assimilation	incentives for mobility and integration with majority community

Stability			Instability
Disruption	*Rebellion*	*Revolution*	*Collapse*
irregular and unsystemic turnover; frequent purges; policy paralysis	power struggles; purges; policy paralysis; competitive elite factions form	multiple "legitimate" elites emerge	no single legitimate national elite is widely recognized
"warnings " military to civilians; broad over-interpretation of orders	barracks revolts, demonstrations, evidence of reluctance to use force against some protesters	coups d'état, joining protesters	civil war; large segments of "national" military split off
petitions, protests, demonstrations, articles, posters	mass protests, strikes, self-destructive protests, fusion of academic and national political issues	leading protests, connect with other groups, mass sustained protests across nation	no national identity; breakdown of national higher educational system
harassment, slow-downs, sabotage, quitting, sit-ins, wild-cat strikes	strikes, both wild-cat and organized, some sympathy actions	general strike; workers joining other social sectors	economic collapse; work without pay
crime and violence, development of organized crime; occasional mob violence	random mob violence	directed mob violence joining and augmenting protests and confrontations	breakdown of law and order; organized crime becomes only dominant force against chaos
hoarding, protests, petitions, non-violent actions	protests, violence, non-payment of taxes, little endurance	sustained rebellion, violence, non-payment of taxes, categorical targeting of enemies	complete lack of commercial agricultural exchange
increase in ethnic identity, resistance to assimilation, occasional ethnic violence	rebellions, increasing intra-ethnic as well as inter-ethnic violence	rebellions are sustained and connected to outside forces	independence for minority areas

2
How Do We Know If China Is Unstable?

H. Lyman Miller

What does it mean to say that a country like China is "unstable"? Some effort at precision in what "stability" and "instability" connote—or at least some attempt to clarify the range of ambiguity—may be useful at the outset.

When we assess the "factors for instability" in a country, what expectations do they convey? Do we mean factors that portend the sudden collapse of the political regime? Systemic change through violent overthrow? Do we include factors that portend transformation of the political order by less than violent means—as in the PRC in 1989, the USSR in 1991, or Indonesia in 1998? Collapse into social and political chaos and civil warfare, as in the former Yugoslavia? Do we include social tensions and political unrest—whether urban riots, worker strikes, peasant uprisings over taxation, ethnic revolts, mass protest movements over corruption and inflation, or large-scale intellectual political dissent and agitation? What about leadership disunity and conflict, as the PRC has seen abundantly since 1949? In the chapters that follow, all of these definitions and criteria are present. In many of them, the implicit definition and criteria of instability shift from one to another and, within single chapters, from paragraph to paragraph.

Instability and Change

How do we differentiate instability from change in general? Usually in hindsight, in the wake of sudden systemic change, factors for instability seem clearer than they did before. How can we distinguish such factors beforehand, apart from those factors and indications of gradual change that may ultimately transform the existing political order but promise to do so in a steady, evolutionary, and above all predictable way?

At first glance, defining instability in terms of stability may seem a promising course. Stability connotes equilibrium, order, and stasis. It conveys the expectation that the way things work now will endure indefinitely. Instability is therefore anything that upsets equilibrium, that renders present order disorderly, or that forces deviation from the expectation that things will continue pretty much as they have been.

From almost any perspective, the dichotomy between stability and instability is hard to get a hold of in contemporary China, and perhaps the effort to locate factors of instability amid a prevailing stability may mislead. What seems overwhelmingly clear is that China today is anything but static, in equilibrium, and orderly. What impresses instead is change, transformation, and motion. Whether the permanence of change in contemporary China also connotes instability is not so clear. There are some basic reasons for this.

From the perspective of comparative politics, change is inherent in communist regimes in at least three fundamental ways that ought to diminish expectations of stability. First, in the early phase of communist regimes, change is inherent in the Communist Party's revolutionary commitment. The Party's explicit mission is social transformation—to shake up the standing social order in a new round of class warfare, and to revise the economic foundations of society—and so is inherently destabilizing.

Second, sooner or later communist regimes confront the necessity of abandoning social warfare in favor of governing, and this change of agenda produces a fundamental crisis of identity. Whether we want to describe this as a crisis of "routinization" as Weber might have, or a shift from a revolutionary to "post-revolutionary" mission, as Richard Lowenthal did, or as the "corruption" of the Party's "heroic" combat mission, as Kenneth Jowitt has done, this shift is inherently destabilizing for the Party, previously the driving force of social transformation.[1] The USSR reached this point in 1961, with the adoption of the 22nd CPSU Congress' program that defined the Soviet Communist Party as a "party of the whole people." In China this stage was reached at the watershed Third Plenum of the Eleventh Central Committee in December 1978, when Deng Xiaoping asserted control over the Party agenda. Reasserting the 1956 Eighth Party Congress line, the Third Plenum communiqué thus authorized promotion of the "forces of production" and raising the overall prosperity of Chinese society—no longer waging class struggle—as the Party's foremost task.

Finally, the commitment of a "post-revolutionary" communist regime to modernization is no less destabilizing because the process of modernization in all societies is socially, culturally, and politically transformative. As Marion Levy advised long ago, modernization is the universal solvent of societies and their traditions, and communist societies, including China, have not been immune from its effects.

Alternatively, from the longer perspective of Chinese history, change has been the norm. From a historically near-term perspective, China has suffered a fundamental crisis of political authority since the collapse of late imperial patterns of governance. With the decline of central authority and the rise of local elite activism in the wake of the Taiping rebellion, the growth of regional self-strengthening elites, and the upsurge in constitutional and revolutionary movements in the late nineteenth and early twentieth centuries, the imperial system gave way to political and military fragmentation and to competing ideological visions of how to reconstitute an enduring political order. The Japanese invasion destroyed any possibility that the Nanjing regime might have succeeded in this, and, despite nearly fifty years tenure, it is not at all clear that the Communist regime will succeed in resolving this crisis of political authority.

The turbulence of China's "modern history" is frequently contrasted in people's minds with the impressive "stability" of the old imperial Confucian order. The roughly 2,000 years of "change within tradition" presented a picture of impressive stability (and implicitly contemptible stagnation), marked by the rise and fall of five or six major dynasties and several short-lived ones, each tracing out similar arcs until the West broke the dynastic cycle and imposed a different course upon the Qing.

A lot depends on periodization, however, and most historians of "premodern" or "traditional" history of China these days have been busy disaggregating the long span of imperial history and no longer accept this periodization. Where one might have demarcated the "Chinese Revolution" following the long conventional historiography, for example, with dates of 1840, 1911, and 1949, a better date for the beginnings of the Chinese Revolution may be 1550, with the commercial expansion of the late Ming period. The economic changes of the mid-sixteenth century set in motion social, demographic, political, and international trends that brought about the withering away of late imperial state and an enduring crisis of political authority that none of the regimes of the twentieth century has been able to resolve. The trends of the post-Mao era in many ways resume those of this longer Chinese revolution, interrupted by the horrific aberration of the Mao period.

Change on the Contemporary Scene

From the perspective of either comparative communist politics or Chinese history, the expectation of stability may be misplaced. If we turn to the contemporary scene, potentially destabilizing change is everywhere. The range and varieties of change are so comprehensive as to be beyond cataloguing. But let me offer five major sectors of change:

- *Transformation of economic order*. As everyone knows, the Deng era has witnessed the gradual, deliberate dismantling of the Stalinist planned economy and restoration of a market economy, together with its attendant anticipated and unanticipated social consequences. Nowadays the Jiang leadership is pressing ahead with state-owned enterprise reform, the most divisive and controversial aspect of this transformation. This reform promises to disenfranchise an entire social class that was previously privileged. Meanwhile new commercial economic elites and economic constituencies are emerging as a product of the economic reforms that want their interests addressed by the political order.
- *Transformation of the Party*. Deng Xiaoping's shift to a post-revolutionary Party agenda has brought about transformation of the Party membership, from top to bottom. Among the top leadership, a generational shift to a "third generation" core leader and collective has coincided with what I have described elsewhere as a shift to a "post-liberation" and "post-revolutionary" leadership.[2] Under this shift, a Deng leadership group that drew heavily from among the Party's founding elite and that dominated politics in the 1980s has given way to a group of leaders around Jiang Zemin most of whom are too young to have participated personally in the revolutionary struggle before 1949 and whose educational credentials and work experience offer the kind of technocratic professionalism suited to the regime's modernization policies. A comparable transformation has occurred in the party rank and file. The most illuminating statistic in this regard was publicized by the Xinhua News Agency on the eve of the Fifteenth Party Congress in 1998, according to which

43 percent of the CPC's 58 million members have some college education. The Party no longer resembles the purposively "proletarian" worker and peasant party it was in Mao's day. Along with these changes, as Bruce Dickson's chapter describes very well, the Party's longstanding institutional roots into society are withering, both in the urban areas as the *danwei* (unit) system dissolves and in the countryside following the marketization of agriculture. Although the Party appears to be using the village election system to try to rebuild its grassroots connections into local rural society, there appears as yet no clearcut approach to doing so in an urban landscape undergoing accelerating change.

- *Transformation of political process*. There have been under way from the beginning of the Deng era concurrent trends toward institutionalization, legalization, and professionalization of politics. In contrast to the unpredictability of institutional processes under Mao's leadership after 1959, Party congresses, Central Committee plenums, and NPC sessions have met precisely according to Party and state constitutional stipulations in the Deng and Jiang periods. The effort to establish legal foundations to regulate all forms of behavior began in 1979 and have only accelerated. Technocrats have won out repeatedly over princelings and factional toadies in the competition for official posts. These changes augur well for stability, although perhaps not necessarily so in all cases. The pattern of strongly bifurcated civil-military leadership described by David Shambaugh recasts a critical relationship onto new foundations; if the concurrent institutionalization of channels between a now overwhelmingly civilian Party leadership and professionalized military leadership cannot constrain the inevitable tensions and frictions between the two, the impact on politics will remain unpredictable.
- *Transformation of political discourse*. Change in the Party and its processes has been abetted by a concurrent withering away of the rhetoric of Marxism-Leninism (what I refer to as "continuing the dissolution under the dictatorship of the proletariat") in favor of a discourse of popular sovereignty. *Jingji ribao* analyses of the state of China's economy and debates on economic reform sound more and more as though they had been written (not coincidentally, perhaps) by World Bank staffers. Foreign policy journals carry analyses of the international situation that are indistinguishable from the writings of hard-core realists at RAND. Even leadership speeches

at authoritative Party occasions can jar one's expectations: Jiang Zemin's exhortation in his political report at the Fifteenth Party Congress last September to China's state enterprise workers to "change their conception of work" to make themselves more competitive sounded more resonant with a *Wall Street Journal* editorial than the words of the general secretary of a proletarian workers' party. In his annual speeches to the United Nations, former Foreign Minister Qian Qichen made no reference to the ideas and words of Marx, Engels, Lenin, Stalin, and Mao, but at least twice he has referred to adages of Confucius.

- *Transformation of state-society relations*. The last two decades have seen a deliberate retreat of the state from society, with the regime tolerating a legitimate private sphere and still limited but nevertheless progressive decontrol of the public sphere. In my view this is finally breaking down the totalizing stance on the relationship between politics and culture for the first time since the May Fourth era and, with it, the iconoclastic attitude toward tradition from the same time. China today, in my view, is not a cultural and ideological vacuum: it is a bewildering riot of competing ideas, values, and re-embraced and frequently reinvented traditions. The outpouring of all of these old and new ideas and values have social constituencies that have made the associational lives of everyday Chinese far richer than at any previous time since 1949. These constituencies bring to public life their distinctive norms and ethos that translate ultimately into ambitions, explicitly or implicitly, for political change. Some of these, as I tried to show with respect to China's dissident scientists in my recent book, are driven by their associational norms to agitate for political liberalism, which may be the best framework for constructively uniting an increasingly pluralistic society.

What Should We Expect?

The scale and depth of these trends invite some simpleminded, straightforward, but perhaps not altogether useless conclusions to bear in mind:

1. *Change, not stability and equilibrium, should be our expectation.* China is not now like it was twenty-five years ago, fifteen years ago, or even five years ago. As rapidly as things seem to move in the present, it is difficult to bear in mind how far things have come. In that regard a

longer perspective than is frequently employed recommends itself—whether from the 20–year perspective of the Deng-Jiang period, the 50–year perspective of the Communist era, the 100–year perspective of China's crisis of political authority, or—to my own eccentric taste—the 400–year perspective of China's long revolution.

2. *The state is not passive.* What has impressed all of us in the past two decades has been the vitality of Chinese society. And with good reason, a lot of the factors of instability are taken as symptoms of a deteriorating Leninist state. But it also bears remembering that the state itself is the initiator—the main author and the conscious agent—of a lot of these trends. In many ways, the deteriorating Leninist state continues to try to remake the economic order, transform society, and ultimately reinvent itself in ways that are not effectively captured by the "stability/instability" dichotomy.

3. *Finally, given the dynamism of the contemporary scene, it is very difficult to determine whether many specific trends are ultimately stabilizing or destabilizing.* Their import is instead ambiguous. Some things that we often cite as factors of instability—corruption, for example—are not clearly so, depending on what perspective we use. The present shift from planned to market economy entails the commoditization and commercialization of exchanges and relations previously defined in other terms, and so reflect a shift in the boundary between "public" and "private" in ways that people may find upsetting but that are not necessarily destabilizing in the long run. The focus on corruption in contemporary China in this regard calls to mind a period of comparable economic and social change that had long-term political impact and that the people of the time found mystifying. Describing the 1840s, Susan Mann and Philip Kuhn wrote:

> Contemporaries frequently explained what was happening in their society in terms of the dichotomy of "public" (*gong*) and "private" (*si*). In their view, the proper realm of public interest, controlled by the government, was shrinking under encroachments from private interests. These included such obvious groups as the patronage networks, salt smugglers and sub-bureaucratic personnel (clerks and runners), who took public resources of the state—and transformed them into sources of private profit. Yet the shift from public to private seems to have been more profound than even these observers realized. Instead of public employment, scholars were now turning to private employment. Instead of using conscripts, the canal system was hiring private laborers. In place of

> the effete hereditary soldiers, the army rolls were increasingly composed of paid militiamen. Tax collectors purchased their grain from private traders; grain tribute administrators leased boats from private shippers. In other words, commercialization as well as corruption, increasing social complexity as well as decadence, were among the factors altering Chinese society and the distribution of power within it, on the brink of modern times. As the monarchy lost its capacity to define its realm against the assertion of private interests, the role of the central government itself in dominating and defining the sphere of public interest was being irreparably damaged.[3]

In this light, contemporary trends may be ambiguous in their longer-term import. Fragmentation may turn out to be pluralization; corruption may be commercialization; and disintegration may be decentralization.

In view of these trends and transformations, despite the impressive cohesion of the Jiang leadership in recent years (or perhaps more accurately, because of it), China seems on the verge of major, possibly systemic change in the near future. No precise, detailed logic of events that leads inexorably to China's democratization on, say, 2:30 P.M. on April 6, 2001, recommends itself. But intuitively the feel of China today—what's being said, how things are said and done—intimates impending change. So is China unstable? If we think in broad terms, of course it is. It seems misleading—and perhaps even foolish—to think of it any other way.

Notes

1. Richard Lowenthal, "Development vs. Utopia in Communist Policy," in Chalmers Johnson, ed., *Change in Communist Systems* (Stanford: Stanford University Press, 1970), 1–32; Richard Lowenthal, "The Ruling Party in a Mature Society," in Mark G. Field, ed., *The Social Consequences of Modernization in Communist Societies* (Baltimore: John Hopkins University Press, 1976), 81–118; Richard Lowenthal, "The PostRevolutionary Phase in China and Russia," in *Studies in Comparative Communism*, Vol.13 No.3 (Autumn 1983), 191–201; and Keneth Jowitt, "Soviet Neotraditionalism: The Political Corruption of a Leninist Regime," *Soviet Studies*, Vol.35 No.3 (July 1983), 275–297, also in Kenneth Jowitt, *New World Disorder: The Leninist Extinction* (Berkeley: University of California Press, 1992), 121–158.

2. See my "The Foreign Policy Outlook of China's 'Third Generation' Elite," in David M. Lampton (ed.), *The Making of Chinese Foreign and Security Policy* (Stanford University Press, forthcoming).

3. Susan Mann Jones and Philip Kuhn, "Dynastic Decline and the Roots of Rebellion," in John King Fairbank, ed., *Cambridge History of China*, Vol.10, Part I, 161–162.

3
The Chinese Leadership: Cracks in the Façade?

David Shambaugh

Chinese communist elite politics have not been known for their stability. A history of endemic factionalism, ruthless rivalries, stealthy maneuver and intrigue, purges, executions, attempted *coup d'etat*, patriarchal politics, and tyrannical dictatorship have all characterized politics at the top of the Chinese political system since the formation of the Chinese Communist Party (CCP) in 1921 and founding of the People's Republic in 1949. To be sure, the post-Mao era witnessed the considerable stabilization of the norms and "rules of the game" for elite politics—yet under Deng Xiaoping factionalism of various kinds continued, senior officials (most notably Hu Yaobang and Zhao Ziyang) were purged from office, patron-client politics were prevalent, and the elite collectively unleashed violent action against its populace in June 1989. Under Deng, however, a considerable degree of normalcy and institutionalization was restored.[1]

Elite politics under Deng's successor, Jiang Zemin, have thus far proceeded remarkably smoothly. The immediate succession to Deng occurred without purges, arrests, or other overt form of factional struggle; a major party congress and three National People's Congresses have been held; the return of Hong Kong went smoothly and various foreign policy initiatives occurred (including two Sino-American summits); and a leadership reshuffle of the Politburo, State Council, and Central Military Commission have all taken place without major disruption.

It thus seems that politics at the top are stable. Is this the case, or is it illusory? Do cleavages exist, and if so over what issues and where in the hierarchy? How serious are they?

The Leadership Balance

The October 1997 15th Party Congress and the March 1998 NPC undertook fairly sweeping personnel changes in the CCP and State Council hierarchies.[2] While the People's Liberation Army (PLA) does not convene a similar regular meeting to confirm personnel changes, the military High Command has also witnessed extensive turnover since 1996.[3] In all three cases recent retirement age regulations are being enforced; this fact alone accounts for a substantial portion of the personnel turnover, although issue preferences and patron-client relations have been additional factors.

The Party Leadership

As a group, the new Party leadership can best be described as technocratic.[4] Nearly all members of the new Politburo possess university training and backgrounds in engineering, electronics, automation, and the like. Eighteen of twenty-four members (and alternates) have university-level technical education (including two trained at the Military Academy).[5] Those who do not have such backgrounds have generally spent their careers working in inner-party or military affairs. Many belong to the generation who began their careers during the 1950s, several receiving training in the Soviet Union during this time. Many worked their way up through the system as economic planners, factory managers, or industrial bureaucrats. Importantly, though, we see in the new Politburo—for the first time—the emergence of the post-Soviet generation: individuals in their fifties, who graduated from universities in China (several from Qinghua University) before and during the Cultural Revolution, and joined the Party during the early 1960s. The socialization of this "fourth generation" of leaders was slightly different than the Soviet-trained "third generation." They are more questioning, open, and perhaps more tolerant of political pluralism.

As technocrats the leaders are, above all, problem solvers. They are not utopian ideologues, bent on remolding society in their vision, nor are they unimaginative bureaucrats seeking only to preserve existing policies, institutional "turf," and their own positions. They recognize

China's myriad problems and are pushing ahead to reform the laggard sectors. They tend to perceive and tackle problems incrementally and in isolation, rather than viewing issues systemically and looking for a comprehensive solution.

With the retirement of Liu Huaqing, Zhang Zhen, and a few others, the Long March generation has fully left *formal* political life. For the most part, it appears that these elders have not been very active behind the scenes—leaving Jiang Zemin & Co. a fairly free hand to manage the Party's and nation's affairs alone. One important exception to this norm has been the continued agitation of elder "leftist" Deng Liqun and his stable of neo-Maoist restorationists. "Little Deng" continues to oversee a mini-publishing and think tank empire of party intellectuals who are, for the most part, critical of the reforms and their effects. Under his auspices (but not authorship), four 10,000 character tracts (*wan yuan shu*) have been published during the past eighteen months, which have been sharply critical of various economic reforms and their socio-political impact. However, since the 15th Party Congress these attacks have waned, Deng's health has declined, and his institutional network is in danger of losing its Party subsidies for their operations.[6] Of the other retired elders who have not died in the last two years, few seem active behind the scenes. One hears occasionally of Song Ping's continued pushing of his crony Hu Jintao's career, or Song Renqiong's continued influence in the Organization Department, but others seem inactive.

The new Politburo also reflects Jiang Zemin's strengthened position. Jiang managed to have a number of his protégés promoted to the Politburo and its Standing Committee. Leaders who must be considered to be in Jiang's network include Li Lanqing and Ding Guan'gen (both of whom he has known since university days in Shanghai), Zeng Qinghong (his longtime staff assistant and most trusted aide), Chi Haotian (the military official whom he has most closely cultivated), Wu Bangguo and Huang Ju (former Jiang deputies in Shanghai), Jiang Chunyun (who he brought to the center to take over the agriculture portfolio at the last Congress), and Hu Jintao (who Jiang seems to be grooming as his eventual successor). Yet, Jiang did not get everything he sought in terms of personnel promotions at the Congress—Chi Haotian was not promoted to the Standing Committee, Zeng Qinghong did not become a full Politburo member, nor was Shanghai mayor Xu Kuangdi elevated to the Politburo. Nor did Jiang succeed in resurrecting the position of Party Chairman and taking this position himself.

Despite these modest setbacks, Jiang undoubtedly strengthened his own power and emerged unrivalled from the Congress. Jiang himself was in the limelight throughout the conclave and clearly emerged from Deng Xiaoping's shadow. Earlier estimates of Jiang as a weak and transitional figure now seem misplaced. Jiang has had to cut deals and make tradeoffs with other leaders—particularly Premier Li Peng and retired General Zhang Zhen—and he clearly has now emerged as China's preeminent leader, but still lacks the authority and vision of Deng Xiaoping.

With Jiang in control and his network in place, this leadership does not show evidence of overt factionalism. High-level infighting or major policy cleavages at the top are not expected, although some individuals (notably Zhu Rongji) evidence potential weaknesses.

The promotion of Zhu Rongji to succeed Li Peng as Premier, with the latter replacing Qiao Shi at the NPC, does constitute a new triumvirate at the pinnacle of power. How these three will relate to each other will have much to do with elite stability or instability in the period ahead. There is some speculation that Jiang is not comfortable with Zhu's assured style and demonstrated ability to speak extemporaneously in public. Many of Li Peng's clients are also not happy about the reorganization of the State Council and many have lost their positions, power, and privileges. Zhu seems to enjoy public popularity, but his base of power in the Party hierarchy is anything but secure. He stepped on many toes to get where he is today and has carved out an agenda of radical restructuring, in which many heads are expected to roll—not usually a recipe for success in Chinese politics. His portfolio of managing the economy in the midst of the Asian financial crisis, and with substantial problems in China's own banking and state industrial sectors, is a high-risk one. He might begin to diversify his portfolio, and there is some evidence that he is doing so in the areas of foreign affairs and science and technology,[7] and this would be to his advantage as one generally has to be a policy generalist to survive at the top of the Chinese leadership system. Further, he seems almost completely devoid of the previously critical factor for upward elite mobility in Chinese politics—*patrons* and *clients*. While he does possess a coterie of economic planners who surround him, Zhu does not possess a network of clients in the party apparatus. More importantly, following Deng's death, he does not seem to have retired elder patrons to support him from behind the scenes (*houtai*). Zhao Ziyang was in a similar position and when his principal patron, Deng Xiaoping, withdrew support, Zhao was exposed, vulnerable, and fell from power. Using this traditional yardstick to measure an elite's security, the lack of strong patrons and loyal clients leaves Zhu Rongji in an extremely vulnerable position should the economy falter (his sole responsibility). Significantly, he has no functional network of bureaucratic allies to fall back on, possesses absolutely no military ties, uncertain relations with Jiang and other elites, and—worst of all—does not have a diversified base of responsibility. Indeed he is riding a real tiger in his one bailiwick: the economy. His brash and decisive style could also cost him. Zhu is not a good horse-trader, compromising politician, or coalition builder—his autocratic style is a definite negative attribute.

For Li Peng's part, he faces the challenge of building a power base in the NPC system while trying to hang on to his ties in the State Council. Li still has considerable seniority as the second ranking leader in the Party hierarchy, and he can use his NPC position effectively, in essence as a veto power over legislation needed by Zhu Rongji to push through his reform and restructuring policies. But, probably for the rest of his career, Li will not be popular with the public and Tiananmen will always haunt him. Should pressure build to "reverse verdicts" on June 4th, Li may be deemed the convenient scapegoat.

Li's power at the NPC and Zhu's in the State Council reflect a continuing dispersion of power away from the Party and military. Policy decisions now increasingly rest in the State Council and Leading Groups, which are largely comprised of functional specialists, while legislation has increasingly become a necessary part of policy implementation.

The State Council Leadership

At the Ninth National People's Congress in March, new Premier Zhu Rongji announced a sweeping overhaul of the State Council. If fully implemented, the overhaul will result in the reduction of ministries and commissions from forty to twenty-nine. This downsizing, however, reflects more the mergers of ministries (thus creating the impression of a net decline) than their elimination. Some energy ministries—such as the Ministries of Coal, Chemicals, Petroleum and Gas—have been abolished and regrouped as bureaus under the new State Economic and Trade Commission. The former State Education Commission and State Science and Technology Commission have been reduced in rank to ministries.

Altogether, the State Council will oversee seventeen bureaus and twenty-odd committees, in addition to the aforementioned twenty-nine ministries and commissions. This streamlining will result in a reduction of State Council bureaucrats from 47,000 to 31,000 (8 million of which are due for redundancy by the end of the year), and perhaps 80,000 more at the provincial and municipal levels.

By any measure, these initiatives represent serious reform. Yet, this is not the first time that the State Council has attempted reduction. Similar initiatives were undertaken in 1982, 1988, and 1993. In each instance, the streamlining plans encountered substantial resistance and the downsizing was more form than substance. Nonetheless, the current initiative promises to pack punch that previous ones lacked.

Zhu has brought to office with him a whole new team of officials. Their appointment marks the rise of the engineering technocrats and hands-on managers in the mold of Zhu Rongji. They are university educated, reasonably cosmopolitan, and largely from coastal provinces. The appointments also reflect the policy priorities of Premier Zhu: banking reform; SOE reform; tax reform; defense industry reform; and reform of China's foreign trade regime to comply with conditions of the World Trade Organization (WTO). Zhu's subordinates in running the economy include several officials who have worked closely with him in recent years—notably newly appointed State Councilor and State Council Secretary General Wang Zhongyu and People's Bank chief Dai Xianglong. But Zhu must also divide labor with Vice Premier Li Lanqing and State Councilor Wu Yi—who are not necessarily in his camp and with whom he has reportedly clashed over economic policy in the past. Additionally, Minister of Defense General Chi Haotian remains loyal to Jiang Zemin and new Foreign Minister Tang Jiaxuan to his patron Qian Qichen. Unlike Li Peng, Zhu is not expected to play any significant role in foreign policy decision making—indeed he did not succeed Li as chairman of the Foreign Affairs Leading Group (Jiang did) and it is not certain that he is even a member of this key body. Further, Zhu's plans to restructure the defense industries, as part of his broader plan to overhaul SOEs will surely meet with resistance in the powerful PLA. There surely exist many other entrenched bureaucratic interests in the State Council—some of which owe personal loyalties to Li Peng and/or others that resist the stripping of their power and resources—that will try and undercut Zhu's reform initiatives.

Thus, Zhu Rongji may be in for rough sailing, because:

- his own personal power base is weak and he has no ties to the military;
- he has to coexist with other senior leaders who do not share his vision of the strategies and tactics of the next stages (or end results) of economic reform;
- many senior and lower-level officials would like to see him stumble for their personal gain;
- many bureaucracies stand to lose status, power, and resources as a result of his restructuring plans;
- the economy is contracting, with exports and foreign direct investment declining;
- the economy is suffering from chronic problems in the financial and state industrial structures, for which there may be no good or cost-effective solution.

As Zhu's reforms bog down and the economy continues to falter, tensions in the State Council and Party leadership are sure to sharpen. If more social instability occurs, the military and security forces may also hold him responsible. Zhu could become an easy scapegoat—although this could have the effect of delaying the very reforms China sorely needs to work through the difficult next stages of reforming the fiscal, state industrial, foreign trade, service, and tax sectors of the economy.

The Military Leadership

As China enters the post-Deng era, the most striking feature of the Chinese military leadership is that it is almost entirely new. With very few exceptions, virtually the entire PLA High Command has assumed their positions within the last two or three years. This includes commanders, deputy commanders, and political commissars of all Military Region commands; all services except the Second Artillery; the General Staff and Logistics Department; the National Defense University and Academy of Military Sciences; the Commission on Science, Technology, and Industry for National Defense (COSTIND); and new General Armaments Department. Even the Central Military Commission has seen nearly half of its membership added since 1995.

The large turnover of leading military personnel is the result of several processes:

- post-Tiananmen shakeups in the officer corps;
- the post-1992 dismantling of the Yang Shangkun/Yang Baibing network;

- the need for successors to replace retiring elder Generals Liu Huaqing and Zhang Zhen, and the promotion of "younger" generals tied to these two;
- increased adherence to retirement age norms and regulations;
- the need to promote more technically competent, combat-experienced, professional officers to guide the PLA's military modernization program; and
- Jiang Zemin's attempts to build a network of senior military personnel loyal to him and the new Communist Party leadership.

With regard to the last point, since Jiang became Chairman of the Central Military Commission he has paid extraordinary attention to garnering support in the PLA High Command,[8] and has personally promoted fifty generals. But it is uncertain that these efforts have necessarily garnered Jiang real allegiance from the new military leadership—indeed most tend to owe their allegiances to military elder Zhang Zhen, new PLA supremo Zhang Wannian, or to no particular individual or faction—but neither is he challenged by them.

Thus the Chinese military leadership is in transition.[9] An entirely new cohort and generation of commanders and military leaders are coming to power. Analysts lack sufficient primary data on the socialization, training, and policy dispositions of the new PLA elite to offer predictions about how they will interact or the nuanced policies they will pursue with a reasonable degree of precision. We know much of the basic data on where they have served, but this is not necessarily a good indicator of the lessons they have learned throughout their careers or the approaches they bring to military modernization or party-army relations at the turn of the century.

Much will depend not only on the socialization of the new military elite, but also on their personal *interaction*. Unlike the previous generation of PLA leaders, the group now emerging at the top have generally not served together for sustained periods of time. They are new to each other, and must establish *modus vivendi* with one another. Some have served together in the military regions or have attended staff colleges together, but this is not the same as the previous generation. Much will also depend on the broader context of party-army relations as well as the amount of revenue made available for military modernization, domestic challenges posed to the military and People's Armed Police by domestic unrest, and external challenges posed by the Taiwan issue, the Korea situation, and the U.S.-Japan security alliance. Importantly, China's new military leadership is largely untested and unproven in managing challenging domestic or foreign crises. The passage of time, and emergence of such crises, will determine the disposition of the new leadership. For the time being, there exist more questions than answers about the new High Command of the PLA. Despite the numerous uncertainties of the new cadre of military leaders, several preliminary characteristics seem apparent.

First, the new military leadership is largely comprised of commanders, warfighters, and soldiers with real and lengthy service experience. Many who have been promoted have actual combat experience from the 1979 Vietnam border war, the 1988 Nansha conflict, the 1969 Sino-Soviet border clashes, the 1962 Sino-Indian conflict, or the Korean War. These individuals all have experience with tactics and strategies related to peripheral defense and are being put in charge of operationalizing the PLA's new doctrine of "limited war under high technology conditions." With a couple of notable exceptions (Chi Haotian, Yu Yongbo), those who have made their careers in the General Political Department (GPD) as political commissars have not advanced into the upper ranks in recent years—while, concomitantly, many who had GPD backgrounds have lost their positions to the "professionals" since the purge of the Yang Baibing network.

Nor, importantly, is the new military leadership comprised of soldier-politicians as in the past—thus severing the previously strong party-army symbiotic link and presenting important implications for understanding the new dynamics of CCP-PLA relations and nothing less than the political future of the PRC. The "interlocking directorate" is definitely being broken, as *no* civilians in the CCP leadership have *any* military experience and very few in the military leadership have experience in the rough-and-tumble world of Zhongnanhai politics (Chi Haotian and Wang Ruilin being the notable exceptions). One therefore expects growing corporatism and professionalism in the armed forces, with the military resisting party encroachment into "army building" as well as party attempts to pull the army in politics or domestic security—but how this becomes manifest in army-party relations is not yet clear. It also raises the issue of constitutionalism and the PLA's relationship to the national "state" as distinct from the ruling party. There is clearly subterranean debate over this issue taking place among intellectuals, party cadre, and military officers. As the PLA is the ultimate guarantor of CCP power, I cannot imagine a *de jure* detachment of army from party control. Nonetheless, it does appear that the armed forces are becoming much more corporate and its interests are growing more autonomous from the Party than at any previous time in its seventy-year history.

Second, having largely spent their careers in regional field commands, the PLA leadership displays a distinctly insular and non-cosmopolitan worldview. With one or two exceptions, they are very poorly traveled abroad (particularly to Japan or the West), know no foreign languages, and presumably have a shallow understanding of the complexities of modernization or modern war. Their exposure to modern warfare and modern armies is virtually nil. There is thus a glaring inconsistency between the backgrounds of the new High Command and the directions in which they are trying to lead the PLA.

Third, the role of military elders has been minimized and will continue to decline (unless there is another crisis akin to 1989 when they may reassert themselves). Elders Zhang Aiping, Li Desheng, and Yang Shangkun have been effectively sidelined from active participation in military politics. Even recently retired Generals Liu Huaqing and Zhang Zhen will likely play little active role in decision making behind the scenes (Zhang more likely than Liu).

Fourth, the new military leadership seems secure in their positions. None display vulnerabilities that could topple them from power in the near term. This is not to say that there will not be portfolio changes, but by not carrying through with expected shifts over the past year the PLA seems content to maintain continuity for the time being. Within a year or two, GPD Director Yu Yongbo will likely retire for reasons of age (watch to see if Wang Ruilin succeeds him); Fu Quanyou may succeed Chi Haotian as Defense Minister, being replaced as Chief of General Staff by Wang Ke, who, in turn, will need a replacement as Director of the General Logistics Department. One should also watch General Cao Gangchuan, the new head of the newly created General Armaments Department, who is also considered a high-flyer, as well as People's Armed Police head General Yang Guoping. PLA supremo Zhang Wannian suffers from ill-defined health problems, which may sideline him in time. He also lives with a couple of skeletons in his closet from his past—having served under Lin Biao co-conspirators Liu Zuopeng and Huang Yongsheng. Zhang is also known to have had close ties to deposed Party chief Zhao Ziyang during the 1960s and again in the 1980s.

Could Leadership Solidarity Crack?

The picture painted above suggests considerable regime unity and coherence. While we did note some potential vulnerabilities—particularly for Zhu Rongji and possibly Li Peng—one must conclude that the Chinese leadership has done a good job of weathering the succession to Deng Xiaoping, as well as undergoing generational turnover and organizational restructuring. To be sure, there is always a high premium placed on leadership "unity and stability" in the CCP, and certainly one principal lesson Chinese leaders derived from the events of 1989 was that elite factionalism can fuel social unrest, cause divisions in army-party relations, and potentially could precipitate an attempted *coup* or even the collapse of the regime. One does not detect the deep cleavages today that have ravaged previous Politburos or precipitated the collapse of communist leaderships in Eastern Europe and the former Soviet Union. *This is not to say, however, that the systemic conditions for Party decay/collapse, or social upheaval, are not present—as I believe they are.*[10] The key question is: How will the Party leadership and government deal with these extant systemic problems (to be addressed in other contributions to this volume) and, if they are unable to stem the tide, how will the military react?[11]

Politics may be stable at the top of the system—but it is not at lower levels. A combination of progressive Party decay, social upheaval precipitated by economic contractions, elite divisions over how to react and a military that is unwilling (at least in part) to intervene, could possibly snowball and challenge the survival of the CCP. There are several key variables that would have to coincide to bring about rapid regime collapse (RRC), not the least of which is the PLA's unwillingness to intervene—as it has several times before—to rescue the Party; but it could happen. Scholars and intelligence analysts would be naïve to the extreme to rule out such a possibility.

More likely than RRC, however, is a slow, methodical, and continued *decay* of the CCP's capacity and legitimacy to rule. The Party has, in this observer's opinion, already lost a considerable degree of both. The malignant cancer of corruption has been a major contributing factor, which has now infested all major organs of the body politic—party, army, state, and society. Despite sincere, but superficial, efforts by the top leadership to control corruption, it has become rooted systemically and institutionally. Further, I would submit that, because of the very nature of *guanxi*, it is sociologically rooted in vast webs of interpersonal relationships which permeate Chinese society. If the decline of ideology corroded the Marxist outer skin of Party legitimacy, corruption has sapped its inner organizational and Leninist strength. With a severe economic downturn, one of the last remaining props of CCP rule will erode. All that will be left is coercion. Social instability spreading across the land, or at least in pockets—represents the signature of all dynastic declines in Chinese history. The use of force to control it is seen in Chinese concepts of governance as profoundly illegitimate (*ba*).

There is ample evidence that the post-Deng leadership is acutely aware of the dangers they face.[12] They are doing what they can to shore up the faltering economy, forestall social unrest, and strengthen the coercive levers of control. Despite recent marginal indications of political loosening, to date they steadfastly resist any significant political reform—which they have concluded, from the East European and Soviet experience, is a slippery slope to extinction. This leaves them in several traps vis-à-vis civil society: they recognize the need, but cannot tolerate truly autonomous civic organizations that may challenge Party hegemony. Of late, they have made a few positive gestures (Bao Tong's release, the exiling of Wang Dan and Wei Jingsheng), have tolerated a moderate degree of intellectual dissent in political discourse (Li Shenzhi's and Sheng Dewen's publications, etc.), and have permitted village elections, but there is apparently no consideration being given to returning to the halcyon reforms of the Zhao Ziyang era—"separation of party and government," creation of a real civil service, strengthening of the NPC, and consideration of subordinating the army to the state instead of the Party, and so on. The very symbol of this period, Zhao himself, remains under house arrest and the ghosts of Tiananmen continue to haunt the leadership.

In sum, politics seem stable at the top, but there are in fact significant cracks in the façade. Do not necessarily expect the regime to collapse or the system to implode soon—but neither should analysts underestimate the severity of the cracks and weaknesses in the system, the potential for considerable social unrest, and the extant depth of Party decay. Radical systemic change will not start at the top of the system, but it will likely end there. The CCP may appear strong on the outside, but it is weak inside. It exhibits many signs of a hollow shell of an organization, one that is unsure of its future, and one that has no positive and persuasive long-term vision for the nation. Pressure from below could paralyze it. Analysts would do well not to assume its indefinite longevity. While policy must be made and governments must deal with the regime in power in Beijing today, policymakers would similarly do well to fully recognize the vulnerabilities confronting the CCP today, and therefore not embrace its leadership too closely. If the Korean and Thai generals, Ferdinand Marcos, and Suharto could be overthrown—to say nothing of former socialist regimes in the Soviet bloc—one should not assume that the CCP and, *ergo*, the PRC will always exist.

Notes

This chapter draws, in part, on my "The Post-Deng Military Leadership," in James R. Lilley and David Shambaugh (eds.), *China's Military Faces the Future* (Armonk, NY and Washington, D.C.: M.E. Sharpe and AEI Press, 1999), and my "Fifteenth Party Congress: Technocrats in Command," *Issues & Studies* (January 1998).

1. See my "The Post-Mao Chinese State," in David Shambaugh (ed.), *The Modern Chinese State* (Cambridge and New York: Cambridge University Press, forthcoming).

2. For further analysis of changes in the Party hierarchy see my "The Fifteenth Party Congress: Technocrats in Command," *Issues & Studies* (Janaury 1998); H. Lyman Miller, "Preparing for Change with Promises of Continuity," *The China Business Review* (January–February 1998); and Richard Baum, "The Fifteenth Party Congress: Jiang Takes Command?" *The China Quarterly* (March 1998). For further analysis of the new State Council leadership see Julie Reinganum and Thomas Pixley, "Bureaucratic Mergers and Acquisitions," *The China Business Review* (May–June 1998).

3. For further analysis of changes in the military hierarchy see my "China's New High Command," *China Review* (Spring 1998), and *China's New Military Leadership: New Faces, New Trends?* (Stanford University Asia/Pacific Research Center, 1998).

4. See Li Cheng and Lynn White, "The Fifteenth Central Committee of the Chinese Communist Party: Full-Fledged Technocratic Leadership with Partial Control by Jiang Zemin," *Asian Survey* (March 1998), pp. 231–64; and Shambaugh, "The Fifteenth Party Congress: Technocrats in Command," *op cit.*

5. This includes: Jiang Zemin (Shanghai Jiaotong University, electrical engineering); Li Peng (Moscow Power Institute, hydroelectric power generation); Zhu Rongji (Qinghua University, electrical engineering); Li Ruihuan (Civil Engineering Institute, architecture); Hu Jintao (Qinghua University, hydraulic engineering); Wei Jianxing (Dalian Institute of Engineering, mechanical engineering); Li Lanqing (Fudan University, industrial management); Ding Guan'gen (Jiaotong University, railway transport); Li Changchun (Harbin Industrial University, electrical engineering); Li Tieying (Charles University, Prague, physics); Wu Guanzheng (Qinghua University, systems dynamics); Chi Haotian (Nanjing Military Academy); Zhang Wannian (Nanjing Military Academy); Luo Gan (Frieberg University, geology and mining); Jia Qinglin (Hebei Engineering College, electrical engineering); Huang

Ju (Qinghua University, electrical engineering); Wen Jiabao (Beijing Geology Institute, geology); Zeng Qinghong (Beijing Engineering Institute, automation); Wu Yi (Beijing Petroleum Institute, degree unknown).

6. Interviews with Deng and members of his network, May 1998.

7. Zhu has become the chairman of the Leading Group on Science, Technology, and Education, and co-vice chairman (with Qian Qichen) of the Leading Group on Foreign Affairs.

8. See my "China's Commander-in-Chief: Jiang Zemin and the PLA," in C. Dennison Lane et al. (eds.), *Chinese Military Modernization* (London and Washington: Routledge, Kegan Paul and AEI Press, 1996).

9. The extensiveness of personnel turnover in the upper echelons of the PLA when one considers, for example Michael Swaine's superb study *The Military and Political Succession in China* (Santa Monica: The Rand Corporation, 1993). Many of the individuals that were prominent in Swaine's study are no longer on the scene, and the centrality that field army-based factional networks played in his analysis has concomitantly declined.

10. For further analysis see Andrew G. Walder, "Does China Face an Unstable Future? On the Political Impact of Rapid Growth," in Michel Oksenberg and Julian Chang (eds.), *China Toward 2020: Social Changes and Political Uncertainty*, forthcoming; and Harvey Nelsen, "The Future of the Chinese State," in Shambaugh (ed.), *The Modern Chinese State*, op cit; Zbigniew Brzezinski, "Disruption without Disintegration," and Arthur Waldron, "The End of Communism," in *The Journal of Democracy* (January 1998), pp. 41–47.

11. For alternative and illuminating analysis of these broad issues, see: David Bachman, "Emerging Patterns of Political Conflict in Post-Deng China"; Frederick Teiwes, "Succession, Institutionalization, Governability, and Legitimacy in the Post-Deng Era"; and Ellis Joffe, "The PLA and Politics: After the Fifteenth Party Congress," papers presented to the conference on "The PRC After the Fifteenth Party Congress: Reassessing the Post-Deng Political and Economic Prospects," Institute for National Policy Research and Mainland Affairs Council, Taiwan, February 1998.

12. On this point see Michel Oksenberg, "China's Political Transformation," in The Aspen Institute, *U.S.-China Relations* (Washington, D.C.: Congressional Program, Vol. 13, No. 2, 1998), p. 25. To quote Oksenberg: "To varying degrees, top officials realize that their political system is antiquated and lacks broad-based popular support. From the highest levels to the lowest, many officials appear to recognize that their regime can only regain popular support through sweeping political reform: strengthening parliamentary bodies, placing the military and policy more firmly under civilian control, relaxing controls over formation of nongovernmental organizations, strengthening the judiciary, improving the civil service system, and granting the populace more meaningful avenues of political participation."

4
Political Instability at the Middle and Lower Levels: Signs of a Decaying CCP, Corruption, and Political Dissent

Bruce J. Dickson

One of the defining features of China's political system has been the preeminent role of the Chinese Communist Party in the political, economic, and social realms. While the CCP maintains a monopoly on legitimate political organization, two decades of reform have weakened its capacity to monitor and control the behavior of not only the vast majority of its citizens but its officials as well. While the party's growing irrelevance in everyday life may benefit economic and social progress, it is also harder for the party to maintain political stability at the local level. The party faces the challenges of party building in the dynamic private sector, of maintaining its control over the newly formed economic and social organizations, and to forestall social demands for political change. Its success in facing these challenges may determine how well it can cope with the prospects of rising unemployment, displaced labor, stagnant or falling standards of living, and the general uncertainty created by the initiation of a new set of reforms at the 15th Party Congress in 1997, and ultimately whether it can preserve China's political stability at a time of rapid economic and political change.

Disintegration of the CCP

With the abandonment of class struggle for the sake of economic modernization, the party shifted its emphasis in recruitment of new members and in the creation of new party organizations. The party now places less importance on its traditional base—workers and peasants—and instead concentrates on intellectual and economic elites. Given the current task of the party, that is an appropriate change in priorities, because intellectual and economic elites have the types of skills and experiences the party needs. Nevertheless, the change in strategy has caused concern among conservatives that the traditional base of the party is being ignored for the sake of formerly "bourgeois" elements. In the past, the party was also "under represented" among workers and peasants, but new recruitment guidelines that two-thirds of new recruits have at least a high school education mean that many workers and peasants do not meet the minimal requirements for membership. The cooptation of technical and economic elites benefits the party's reform program, but also means it is less embedded in lower strata of society.

In addition, little new recruitment is taking place in the non-state sectors of the economy. On the one hand, new enterprises are being created too rapidly and in numbers too large for the party to build basic level organizations in them. Managers of these enterprises, especially joint ventures, are not enthusiastic about party building in their enterprises. On the other hand, many of the workers in these enterprises are mobile, moving from one enterprise to another and even one city to another with some frequency. This gives the local party committee less time to identify and recruit them into the party. In addition, these workers are motivated by the promise of higher wages, and see party membership as adding additional burdens to their lives with few benefits. As a consequence, the party is poorly represented and organized in the most dynamic part of the economy.

Even in the state sector, the party is less active on the shop floor than in the Maoist era. Recent scholarship on labor politics bear little resemblance to the neo-traditionalism depicted by Walder.[1] The manager, not the party secretary, is in charge of the factory, and there is little evidence of political education or mobilization among the work force. Instead of intentionally creating divisions among the workers as a tool of control, the divisions are now vertical, between labor and management. The party organization seems to play little part in factory politics at present.

Party members within the floating population create particular difficulties for the party. Although they are supposed to register with the party committee in whatever city or town they currently reside, few do.

Local party committees would like these floating party members to pay dues, attend party life meetings, abide by party discipline, and set an example for others, but the floating party members have other priorities. Like the rest of the floating population, they are motivated by material incentives and not by the party's traditional appeals.

With the steady decay of the party's authority and organization, so-called feudal influences have reemerged in many areas of China. Clan-based lineages are once again influential in many rural areas. They often enjoy wide support locally, and can be involved in criminal activity, such as drugs, smuggling, or kidnapping. In some areas, they have reportedly replaced the party as the center of power, and in other areas party and government leaders are themselves clan members. The decline of the CCP at the local level has also contributed to the spread of religion, both the resumption of traditional religions, such as Buddhism, Taoism, and ancestor worship, and also to renewed interest is Christianity. Central policy in this regard is less important than the attitude of local leaders. Some see these trends as a threat to the state's and their own personal authority and try to clamp down. The 1999 crackdown on the Falun Gong sect was indicative. Reports of repressive measures seem to be most prominent in the inland, less developed areas. In the more developed coastal provinces, there are reports of local leaders taking more conciliatory measures. Rather than try to stop the spread of clans and churches, some local leaders try to forge alliances with clan and church leaders in order to preserve the peace and to implement mutually beneficial policies, especially the provision of medical and welfare services to the poor, elderly, and disabled. Some even see increased religious activity as an opportunity to make money, by renting unused office space to churches or lending money for the building of new churches. The Western media and political activists often portray a one-sided portrait of repressive religious policies in China, but the reality is more diverse.

Are these examples of the disintegration of the CCP at the local level signs of decay of the political system as a whole, or simply indicators of its evolution toward a less monolithic polity? We should not be nostalgic for the days when the CCP was in a more domineering position. When the party recruited large numbers of peasants and workers, it also tended to pursue more radical policies that did more harm than good to both the society and the economy. The party may have enjoyed greater control over the workplace during the Maoist era, but its actions did not lead to efficient use of labor in production or raise standards of living for the workers. Not all clans are local Mafia, and the use of familial networks for political, economic, and social mobility is common among party leaders, as it is in many cultures and political systems. Clan and religious leaders may detract from the authority of local officials, but many local officials are themselves tyrants with little regard for the local population.

The CCP itself is aware of these various trends and has taken steps to accommodate some of them. Recognizing that the transition from class struggle to economic reform requires concomitant changes in its organization and personnel, it has tried to adjust to the new environment, although with mixed results. It has adopted a coordinated strategy to coopt the newly emerging economic and technical elites and to build corporatist style institutions to better link state and society, especially in the economic realm. In addition, it has promoted village level elections as a means to make local leaders more accountable, more popular, and as a result better able to implement mandated reform policies.

Rather than target labor, the party now concentrates its energies on college students and the owners and managers of non-state enterprises. Although communist ideology has been in decline for the better part of two decades, and the CCP's role in everyday life has declined over the same period of time, membership in the party has continued to grow. Today roughly 58 million people are members of the CCP (about 4 percent of the total population). Many new members are among the best educated and most economically successful businessmen in the country. It may seem an anomaly that such people are interested in joining the party, but party membership still provides a variety of benefits. For young people interested in administrative positions, either in the government bureaucracy or in state owned enterprises, a party card—in combination with a college degree—is a prerequisite for career advancement.[2] These may not be the most talented of their generation, but enough advanced university students still find advantages in party membership that recruiters have little difficulty finding new members for the party.

Even though the party's traditional ideology and continued pledge to promote socialist goals may not inspire many students and businessmen, party membership still offers a variety of tangible rewards to them. As long as the CCP remains the ruling party, it will find new members. Increased membership, however, is no guarantee of vitality. Many new recruits join solely for the material rewards and do not attend party meetings or have further commitment to the party's larger goals (other than economic growth). Loyalty to the party, even among its own members, probably does not run very deep.

Despite the trend toward a market economy, the government is still very much involved in the economy. Close government-business relations is a key to local economic success. China has a more cooperative arrangement between government and business, as in other Asian countries, unlike the adversarial relationship in the United States. One way of forging a close working relationship is to coopt successful businessmen into the political system. The CCP recruits many successful businessmen: surveys report 15–20 percent of private entrepreneurs are party members, as compared to 5 percent of the overall population. My survey of large and medium scale private entrepreneurs found 40 percent of them were party members![3] Central policy bans this practice because of the very correct idea that capitalists do not belong in a communist party, but local leaders need the skills and prestige of entrepreneurs.[4] So they get around the ban by saying they are not "private" entrepreneurs in a strict sense, but only managers of joint stock or collective enterprises, or by simply ignoring the ban. For businessmen, party membership provides access to essential business needs as loans, licenses, and the cooperation of the local officials. It also provides more direct access to decision-making circles and helps maintain the local state's commitment to economic growth.

In order to further extend its influence over the rapidly growing nonstate sector of the economy, the state has also created several business associations for local businessmen, depending on the size of the enterprise and whether it is privately owned, a joint venture, a joint stock company, etc.[5] These associations have limited autonomy—their leaders are often drawn from the government agencies that regulate the economy, local officials see their primary purpose as upholding party leadership over the private sector, and asserting the interests of businessmen toward the state is a decidedly secondary purpose. However, they are not merely "transmission belts" for the state either. In my survey of entrepreneurs and local officials, 87.7 percent of the businessmen who sought the help of business associations to solve business and other problems said the associations had been helpful (28.8 percent said they were very helpful, and 58.9 percent said they were a little helpful), and 44.5 said business associations can influence the local implementation of policies (on the other hand, only 18.8 percent of local officials agreed with this statement). As is so often the case, the more resources a business association controls, the more influence it has with the local government.[6] For instance, the business association whose members provide a large number of jobs, large fixed assets, large sales, and more tax revenue, get more leeway than do small shop owners or street vendors. But activities of business associations have been limited to economic policy. They have shown little interest in promoting political change.

In the United States, many people portray private entrepreneurs as vehicles of political change, but they may be betting on the wrong horse. Entrepreneurs are partners with the state in China, and are unlikely to be the source of political opposition in the near future. Economic development may ultimately lead to political change in China, but the link between economic change and political change is very loose. Businessmen who are promoting and benefiting from economic growth may be in favor of opening up the policy process so that the interests of businessmen and other experts are incorporated, but they are generally not advocates for democracy.[7]

A second type of institution that is building is the spread of village level elections, which has received a fair amount of scholarly and media attention in recent years, especially among those who hope that the institutionalization of local elections will prove to be the first step toward democratization.[8] However, it is not clear how wide spread these elections are (reports range from 10 to 85 percent of villages holding successful elections), and reports persist of cadre interference in the campaigns and results, including disqualifying candidates, limiting the number of candidates to one per office, and the nullification of results. In contrast, there are numerous reports of truly "meaningful" elections, in which there were multiple candidates, where the elected leaders were not hand picked by higher level party leaders, and where leaders became more accountable to villagers. The CCP has often complained that its grass roots leaders are out of touch with the masses, and elections provide one means of correcting that problem.

Despite the large number of case studies of local elections, there seems to be no relationship between meaningful elections and such things as local standards of living, rate of growth, level of literacy, etc. What matters most is not these standard measures of modernization, but instead the attitude of local party and government leaders, which is hard to predict. Elections have been most successful where township and county leaders are supportive of elections and increased political participation.

As in many policy areas, support of local officials is the prerequisite for successful implementation of these election reforms.

Elections are not intended to allow opposition to the communist party or to promote alternative policies. Those who try to do so are prevented from running for election and if elected they are prevented from taking office. Instead, elections serve two functions. First, public relations: foreigners love elections, and a number of delegations from the United States and Europe have monitored elections and come away impressed. At a time when China faces criticism on a host of other political and economic issues, this is one area where it earns applause. Second, facilitate policy implementation: candidates cannot promise to cut taxes or to relax the one-child policy, but they can promise to make the implementation of those policies fairer and better understood. Where meaningful elections have taken place, implementation of these unpopular policies has gone smoother.[9] But these are instrumental rationales for popular elections, and do not indicate a deeper belief in the principles that underlie democratic rule. Advocates of popular elections must confront the widespread belief, among both China's leaders and its citizens, that the country is too poor and its people too poorly educated for successful democratic rule.[10]

Elections are not a vehicle for political opposition, but they are a channel for political participation. In some villages, successful businessmen have converted their economic success into political power by running for office. Promising to pay villagers higher dividends from collective enterprises has tremendous appeal. It is not yet clear if these entrepreneurs turned politicians have a larger agenda, or even if they are developing horizontal communication networks to coordinate efforts and share information. Perhaps to forestall such efforts, and to prevent popularly elected leaders from being outside its reach, the CCP coopts winners of elections if they are not already party members. In fact, 68.9 percent of the businessmen and 64.7 percent of the local officials in my survey agreed that if a private entrepreneur is elected as village leader but is not already a party member, he should join the party. To be influential, one must be "within the system" (*tizhi nei*); in China's political system, autonomy is not the result of remaining aloof from the party but in controlling resources that are not dependent on the party's provision.

Both the cooperative government-business relationship and the spread of village level elections are stabilizing factors, but they are also double-edged swords. As local business associations become more autonomous and wield more influence, and as China's citizens get more accustomed to voting, they may expect their leaders to be more accountable and more responsive. That may ultimately put pressure on central leaders to consider the types of political reforms that they have so far been unwilling to undertake.

Decentralization and Its Consequences

The economic reform initiatives of the post-Mao era entailed a reduction of central control over both economic and social activity. This decentralization of authority contributed to the rapid growth of China's economy, but has also made the center less able to mandate and monitor the behavior of local leaders, because local leaders now control a greater share of the economic resources and they do not have to be loyal agents of the center in order to be successful. The center must therefore cajole, persuade, and negotiate with local leaders to get its way. For example, there has been widespread resistance to new tax policies, to new limits on unbudgeted investment, and efforts to fight local protectionism. In addition, the emergence of markets in the post-Mao era also provided the ways and means for workers and farmers to attain the necessary goods and services for daily life, reducing their dependence on factory managers and party and government officials. In short, by reducing the center's control over the economy, lower level officials, and members of society, the introduction of markets undermined the "institutional pillars" of a communist system. And as the state's ability to monitor compliance and sanction behavior is reduced, the stability of the political system itself declines.[11]

The trend of declining central authority has created concern by some observers that China is on the brink of collapse or a return to warlordism.[12] I think this concern is overblown, because there are off-setting stabilizing factors (most prominently the centuries' old tradition of a unified China and the dominance of the Han nationality in most areas of China) and because decentralized authority can moderate the swings of political sentiment at the center (as when central leaders tried to roll back reforms in the early 1990s). But the decentralization of authority does contribute to the fears of political instability if the center cannot coordinate and implement effective responses to recurring episodes of local protest over the economic and social changes now underway.

One consequence of weakened central authority has been the explosion of corruption among party, government, and military leaders at all levels. The unchecked spread of corruption is a clear manifestation of the center's inability to monitor and control the behavior of provincial and local officials. Although the level and scope of corruption is hard to measure accurately, media reports suggest that the number of investigations and punishments grow with every passing year. Apparently, the benefits of corruption still outweigh the risk of exposure. The institutions created to handle this problem—the Central Discipline Inspection Commission, the Ministry of Supervision, and their local offices—do not have the manpower, the resources, or the elite support needed to turn this problem around. In fact, corruption has become so severe that some people speak nostalgically of the days of Nationalist China or the Maoist era. Such sentiments reflect how frustrated some people have become with the current situation. But the situation shows no sign of improving.

For over a decade, central leaders have identified corruption as the greatest threat to the survival of the CCP and to the current regime. They have taken efforts to address the corruption issue, but to no avail. It faces a dilemma in this regard: exposing cases of corruption also reveals the depth and magnitude of the problem. The vast majority of cases target leaders at and below the county level; with the exception of a few prominent cases, such as former Beijing party secretary Chen Xitong, provincial and central officials have rarely been punished. Even the sons and daughters of central leaders (the *gaogan zidi*) are able to flout the law and engage in a variety of corrupt endeavors, including real estate deals, fraudulent service contracts, and foreign trade deals. Resentment against this type of behavior was reportedly one reason why members of the "princelings faction" were kept off the Central Committee at the 15th Party Congress.

At the local level, corruption has various consequences. As is often noted, corruption can be beneficial. It is grease for the wheels of an imperfect and undeveloped market, allowing enterprises to avoid market distorting regulations and get the inputs, licenses, access to loans, transportation and markets they need to conduct business. There is also reportedly popular support for petty corruption to provide a little extra income for underpaid local officials, so long as they promote local well-being. But corruption threatens political stability when it does not contribute to economic growth but instead contributes primarily to private gain. The threat is not so much protests directly against corrupt officials, but the gradual but steady gnawing away of legitimacy and support for the political system as a whole. Cases of high level corruption, for instance involving real estate and foreign trade deals, undermine popular support for the regime even when individual citizens are not personally damaged. Resentment against corruption contributed to popular support for the 1989 demonstrations, although by itself was not enough to trigger the protests. So long as the public perceives that the benefits of growth are being unfairly eaten up by unproductive and unaccountable leaders, corruption diminishes respect for authority and adds to the list of grievances felt against the state, thus having a contagious effect when protests do break out.

Corrupt practices by local officials have also led directly to isolated political protests which pose a threat to political stability more generally. For instance, local officials occasionally have been forced to pay for grain from farmers with IOUs because they have misspent the money allocated for grain purchases. During the early 1990s, this led to direct protests by local farmers against the government in a variety of locales, threatening political stability in those areas. Whether corruption leads to direct protests or simply the continued deterioration of popular support, it poses one of the major problems facing central and local governments in maintaining political order.

Political Dissent

Political dissent in China occurs on both extremes of the political spectrum: from those who believe the current trajectory of economic reform fails to address the structural problems that allow labor abuses, corruption, and malfeasance to prosper, on the one hand, to those who believe those same reforms have betrayed the revolution and must be abandoned. The former complaint generally comes from outside official channels without any legitimate means of dissemination and is generally seen as more of a threat to the state than the latter viewpoint, which has several officially sanctioned journals to publish and distribute its concerns. As in the Maoist era, it is still safer to be on the "left" than on the "right" in China. The leftist critiques, identified with Deng Liqun and his small band of adherents, probably has too little popular appeal to bother with. Efforts to repress dissent therefore concentrate on demands for liberalization and democratization.

The legacy of Tiananmen is more important in the West, and especially in the United States, and especially in Washington, D.C., than it is in China. In the United States, the word "Tiananmen" is a symbol for repression of democratic yearnings, of the slaughter of innocents. That is because most Americans were unaware of the word or the place before spring of 1989. But Tiananmen has been the focal point of political activity for decades in China, much as the Mall is the symbolic political center of the United States. It is the place where protestors have demonstrated against their government (as in the May 4 movement of 1919, the protests against Cultural Revolution policies following the death of Zhou Enlai in 1976, and the democracy movement of 1989). It is the place where governments have mobilized their supporters (as in 1949 when Mao Zedong announced the founding of the People's Republic of China after a long civil war, in 1966 and 1967 when Mao presided over large gatherings of Red Guards, and in 1997 when the government celebrated the return of Hong Kong to Chinese sovereignty). It is the place where governments meet foreign leaders, as occurred in June when President Clinton began his summit meeting with Jiang Zemin and other Chinese leaders. Criticism of Clinton's agreement to be received at Tiananmen was silly—it shows how little American politicians and media understand the political sites and symbols of China.

That said, it is also true that the official verdict on the spring 1989 demonstrations, that they were a rebellion, not a patriotic movement, remains a stumbling block to certain types of political reform and political action. There are periodic calls for "reassessing the verdict," most prominently by Zhao Ziyang at the time of the party congress last fall and again on the eve of Clinton's visit, but so far to no avail. The leaders recognize that to change the verdict would be to legitimize large scale, organized protests against the state for the sake of political change, and that is not something they are willing to consider at this time. For most Chinese, Tiananmen seems a distant memory, forgotten in the rush to economic gain. In fact, many intellectuals have reluctantly come to the conclusion that the crackdown, and the reassertion of political control, was a prerequisite for economic growth. The contrary examples of the former Soviet Union and the former communist countries of Eastern Europe reinforce their perception of the need for political control to maintain stability and therefore economic development.

"It's the economy, stupid." With economic growth creating rising standards of living and expanding opportunities, satisfaction (or perhaps just complacency) is high. In casual conversations, there is little interest in politics. Any political explosion in the near term is as likely to be the result of labor unrest than political dissatisfaction with the political system as a whole. Threats to economic well-being are a bigger threat to political stability than are the frustrated political ideals of China's dissidents. Consequently, demands for independent labor unions are a prominent part of many dissenting voices. Whether this is a sincere aspiration or a tactical effort to arouse public support is hard to determine. In any event, the state has not shown any indication it is willing to allow independent unions. To sever the party's link to organized labor would be particularly dangerous at this time of uncertainty.

Since the conclusion of the Clinton-Jiang summit and the 15th Party Congress in the fall of 1997, repression of dissidents in China has been less systematic. The relaxed international environment, especially relations with the United States, and the CCP's renewed commitment to reform makes China's leaders less sensitive to societal demands for further reform and therefore less prone to crack down on each call for change. In 1997 not only were prominent dissidents such as Wei Jingsheng and Wang Dan released into exile, but some dissidents calling for independent unions, or political reform, remained out of jail. This temporary loosening tightened in 1998-99 with the crackdown on China Democratic Party activists and Falun Gong sect adherents. As is the norm in contemporary China, every hint of a new beginning is accompanied by examples of the familiar old practices. While there has not been a complete transformation in China's policy toward dissent, there have been indications of a partial change nonetheless.

As a consequence, China is experiencing a more liberal environment right now. Chinese scholars describe the current period as the most open in memory, completely out of synch with the general perception in the West. The Western media has also begun reporting on this most recent political thaw, but without the enthusiasm that accompanied higher profile movements in 1978–79 and 1989. There are still political prisoners and new arrests. There are limits on what can be said and published. But there are also calls for political reform and adherence to law that go unpunished. Most calls are for fine-tuning the system to make it more efficient, not an overhaul of the system and rearranging the balance of power between the main political institutions or between state and society. For instance, the unchallenged authority of the CCP is generally not an issue, except to mirror the official line that party cannot and should not micro manage all affairs, especially when it comes to business. In general, there is optimism among establishment intellectuals about the adaptability and durability of the current system.

Dissidents promoting democratic progress and respect for human rights face not only government opposition but also the skepticism of broad segments of Chinese society. Without better public opinion surveys, it is impossible to know the current beliefs of Chinese citizens, but most observers agree that fears of political chaos are quite strong. Correctly or not, many Chinese fear that the promotion of individual liberties and free speech that are the basis for international norms of human rights are not consistent with Chinese traditions and more importantly pose the risk of political instability in the here and now that threaten continued economic development. Like many authoritarian governments, China's leaders have argued there is a tradeoff between the goal of economic development and international norms of human rights, which they argue would threaten the nation's stability and slow its growth. In order to maintain stability and promote growth, they argue, dissent must be held in check. This rationale seems to resonate with many of China's citizens. Some have wondered why the Western nations, and the United States in particular, seem so interested in the fates of the few thousand political prisoners when the living standards of hundreds of millions of Chinese are improving. While there need not be such a tradeoff between human rights and stability, the debate in China often is oversimplified that way. Political dissidents in China therefore have to confront not only potential repression by the state but also deep rooted cultural norms.

Efforts by China's dissidents to mobilize popular support are hampered by the CCP's monopoly on political organization, which it guards zealously. For instance, there is no group like Charter 77 in Czechoslovakia or other Eastern European organizations which organized the activities of and spread information among dissidents before the collapse of communism. "Virtual networks" of dissidents may be spreading throughout China via the Internet. The Chinese government has tried various measures to monitor and regulate the flow of information on the Internet in China, but the versatility of the web makes this difficult. It also makes it difficult for outside observers to assess the scope or efficacy of such communications.

The absence of organized opposition makes political protest so unpredictable in China, and so explosive and prone to excess when it does occur. The "rules of the game" are a bit clearer than in the late 1980s, the last period of political ferment, but the boundaries of the permissible are still shifting. Journals and publishers are always uncertain regarding how far is too far. While groups with varying degrees of autonomy do exist, such as local chambers of commerce, they have not been used as a vehicles for political protest or opposition.

Conclusion

As a consequence of the trends outlined above, the prestige of party membership has declined. Party membership is still valuable, especially for those seeking administrative careers, either as cadres or managers. But for others, party membership is no longer the sole avenue toward high paying and prestigious careers. Other avenues, in particular higher education and private entrepreneurship, separately or in tandem with a party card, provide alternate career paths. The CCP is therefore less visible in everyday life, less consequential to and less able to maintain political stability. These problems when compounded by other factors not covered in this paper, such as rising unemployment, the absence of a social safety net, and the uncertain outcomes and costs of the current reform initiatives, threaten the CCP's inability to address and cope with the outpouring of social demands.

The economic reforms of the post-Mao period have rapidly transformed China's economy and society, but have had generally negative consequences for the CCP. In rural areas, it is barely operational, staffed with old men, unable to attract new recruits, and forced to compete with local clans and churches for influence. In the dynamic private sector, it is also poorly represented because it has not been able to build party organizations or recruit new members fast enough to keep pace with the explosion of new firms. It has ceded many of the powers it enjoyed in the past to factory managers and local government officials. Even though these managers and officials are usually themselves party members, the party as a separate political institution is becoming less relevant in the lives of most Chinese and less effective in carrying out its policies.

The decline of the CCP at lower levels was a corollary of the post-Mao reform agenda and has had a variety of beneficial consequences. But disintegration is not adaptation. Although it has shown it can get out of the way of economic and social progress, it has not yet demonstrated what role—if any—it can perform in the rapidly changing domestic environment its policies have created. In the short run, the CCP has a number of features that will likely allow it to survive. It still has a monopoly on political organization, which makes it difficult for any opposition to mobilize effectively against it. It provides a number of material advantages to its members and can still attract intellectual and economic elites. In other countries, these elites pose a potential threat to the state, but by coopting them the CCP minimizes their threat. And the general improvement in living standards creates a veneer of legitimacy, even though questions of economic inequality and corruption can easily break the surface.

But over the long run, the fate of the party is less certain. The CCP in the past has been unable to tolerate demands for political reform that emanate from society, and because there are few autonomous social organizations, it has not been possible to negotiate a political reform agenda. An explosive situation could therefore develop under a variety of circumstances:

- if the newly created business associations begin to take on political issues;
- if China's citizens become accustomed to local elections and come to expect more accountability from all their leaders;
- if the new efforts to reform the state owned enterprises and the bureaucracy prove too disruptive;
- if the Asian financial crisis spills over into China and economic growth nosedives;
- or if the scattered strikes and protests begin to snowball or become linked together.

China's current political institutions are not designed to respond to social pressures: indeed, they were designed to change society, not adapt to it. A revolutionary situation could quickly and unexpectedly develop—as it did in 1989 and in early 1998 in Indonesia—and if it does, we are likely to see either repressive steps to restore order or a prolonged period of instability and uncertainty that could spill over into neighboring countries. For the time being, stability may prevail in China, but it is a fragile stability. When fundamental political change does come about, it is likely to be sudden and tumultuous, not gradual and incremental.[13] This is the scenario most disturbing to stability in Asia more generally and to U.S. interests, but given recent trends in China and elsewhere it is a scenario that cannot be ignored.

Notes

1. Andrew G. Walder, *Communist Neo-Traditionalism: Work and Authority in Chinese Industry* (Berkeley: University of California Press, 1986).

2. See Erik Eckholm, "At China's Universities, A Rush To Party, as in Communist," *New York Times*, January 31, 1998.

3. In the fall of 1997, I conducted a survey of private entrepreneurs and local party and government officials in three counties (one each in Hebei, Shandong, and Zhejiang). The questions focused on the personal and institutional relationships between entrepreneurs and officials, and also on the basic political beliefs of both groups. Some of the preliminary results are reported in this paper.

4. Sixty percent of local officials in my survey agreed that private entrepreneurs have the types of skills the party now needs. An even higher percentage of entrepreneurs felt the same way: 78.8 percent. Whether an entrepreneur was a party member or no significant difference made little difference on this question. In fact a slightly higher percentage of non-members (79.6) than party members (76.6) agreed with the statement.

5. Gordon White, Jude Howell, and Shang Xiaoyuan, *In Search of Civil Society: Market Reform and Social Change in Contemporary China* (Oxford: Oxford University Press, 1996); Jonathan Unger and Anita Chan, "Corporatism in China: A Developmental State in an East Asian Context," in Barrett L. McCormick and Jonathan Unger, eds., *China after Socialism: In the Footsteps of Eastern Europe or East Asia* (Armonk, NY: M.E .Sharpe, 1996).

6. Christopher Earle Nevitt, "Private Business Associations in China: Evidence of Civil Society or Local State Power," *China Journal*, no. 36 (July 1996), pp. 25–45.

7. For the views of China's entrepreneurs (in particular their reactions to the 1989 democracy movement) see Margaret Pearson, "The Janus Face of Business Associations in China: Socialist Corporatism in Foreign Enterprises," *Australian Journal of Chinese Affairs*, no. 31 (January 1994), pp. 25–46; and David Wank, "Private Business, Bureaucracy, and Political Alliance in a Chinese City," *Australian Journal of Chinese Affairs*, no. 33 (January 1995), pp. 55–71.

8. Lianjiang Li and Kevin J. O'Brien, "The Struggle Over Elections," in Roderick MacFarquhar and Merle Goldman, eds., *The Paradox of China's Reforms* (Harvard University Press, 1999); Steven Mufson, "China Dabbles in Democracy to Run Villages, Reform Party," *Washington Post*, January 26, 1995.

9. For further details, see Daniel Kelliher, "The Chinese Debate over Village Self-Government," *The China Journal*, no. 37 (January 1997).

10. For an account of efforts by Wang Zhenyao, until recently in charge of village level elections at the Ministry of Civil Affairs, see Steven Mufson, "A Quiet Bureaucrat Promoting the Vote One Village at a Time," *Washington Post*, June 14, 1998.

11. Andrew G. Walder, "The Quiet Revolution from Within: Economic Reform as a Source of Political Decline," in Walder, ed., *The Waning of the Communist State: Economic Origins of Political Decline in China and Hungary* (Berkeley: University of California Press, 1995).

12. See, for instance, Jack A. Goldstone, "The Coming Chinese Collapse,"

Foreign Policy, no. 99 (Summer 1995), pp. 35–52; for a rebuttal, see Yasheng Huang, "Why China Will Not Collapse," *Foreign Policy*, no. 99 (Summer 1995), pp. 54–68.

13. I have elaborated on this point elsewhere; see *Democratization in China and Taiwan: The Adaptability of Leninist Parties* (London and New York: Oxford University Press, 1997); and "China's Democratization and the Taiwan Experience," *Asian Survey*, April 1998.

5
Sources of Macroeconomic Instability in China

Nicholas R. Lardy

The greatest source of macroeconomic instability in China is its weak financial system.[1] This linkage is evident at several levels. Macroeconomic fluctuations over the past two decades have been quite marked, in part because a weak financial system has constrained the development of effective monetary policy instruments. Second, China is currently extremely vulnerable to an economic slowdown that could place significant pressure on its banking system. Finally, the rapid build up of bank credit and a significant deterioration of loan quality creates the possibility of a financial meltdown.

Lack of Effective Monetary Policy Instruments

A principal reason for the substantial macroeconomic fluctuations that have marked the reform era, which began in 1978, is the absence of effective monetary policy instruments. In periods of relative price stability credit has been readily available to state-owned firms and loans outstanding from both banks and other financial institutions rise rapidly. The resulting increased levels of investment and more rapid growth of the wage bill stimulates inflation, leading eventually to a period of credit tightening as the authorities attempt to rein in inflationary pressures. But tightening of credit has come through the imposition by the People's Bank of China of lower credit quotas on state-owned banks and other administrative controls, rather than through higher real interest rates.

Indeed, since the central bank has adjusted nominal lending rates they require banks to charge borrowers relatively slowly during inflationary periods, the real lending rate tended to be falling when the government's credit policy turned contractionary.

The People's Bank of China recognizes that to moderate macroeconomic fluctuations more effectively it must shift to greater reliance on indirect instruments of monetary control, especially adjustment of bank liquidity through open market operations and other measures to control excess reserves of banks. The bank set the stage for open market operations in 1993, when it issued central bank bills to absorb excess liquidity. Although the bank planned to begin genuine open market operations in 1994, it was forced to postpone this initiative, largely because it was unable to allow greater interest rate flexibility.

Further movement in the direction of greater reliance on indirect monetary policy instruments was evident in 1998 when mandatory credit quotas for the largest state-owned banks were eliminated. The central bank, however, is continuing to issue quarterly "guidance credit plans" to influence both the magnitude of total lending as well as the sector distribution of loans of the largest banks. Ultimately, the effective use of open market operations will require not only the phasing out of all lending guidance to banks but much greater flexibility of interest rates on lending, a greater sensitivity of banks to costs, and on further reforms in the enterprise sector that increase the sensitivity of firms to the interest rate they pay on loans.

Over Leveraged Firms

Because they have borrowed excessively over a sustained period, Chinese firms now have debt to equity ratios that are among the highest in the world. In 1995 the average state owned firm had almost six times more debt than equity, a ratio that exceeds that found in the highly leveraged Korean chaebol. One shortcoming of such a high debt to equity ratio is that in economic downturn the sales of most firms will fall and profits will fall even more rapidly. Thus, profits of an increasing share of firms likely will fall below the level necessary simply to pay interest on their debts. That, in turn, will place enormous pressure on an already fragile banking system. Their rate of return on assets, already quite depressed, likely will fall further, undermining the efforts of the central government to restore the capital adequacy of the large state-owned banks to the levels specified in the Basle Accord. That, in turn, almost certainly will undermine the government's program to require the banks to operate on commercial principles.

A Banking Crisis?

The most serious threat to macroeconomic stability in China is the possibility of a domestic banking crisis. The central precondition for a crisis, a largely insolvent banking system, already exists. Loans have grown at an extraordinary pace for twenty years, while asset quality has declined sharply. Loans outstanding from all financial institutions in China increased almost forty-fold, from RMB 190 billion at year-end 1978 to RMB 7.5 trillion at year-end 1997. Relative to the size of the economy loans doubled over this period and by year-end 1997 were fully equal to gross domestic product.

At the same time the quality of the loan portfolios of most Chinese financial institutions has deteriorated dramatically. The best data are for the four largest state-owned banks, which at year-end 1995 accounted for three-fifths of the assets of all financial institutions in China. Their nonperforming loans, as a share of total loans, increased from 20 percent at year-end 1994 to 25 percent at year-end 1997. Moreover, the share of nonperforming loans that is accounted for by the most impaired categories of loans has increased. Specifically, the sum of the share of loans that are outstanding to firms that have already gone through bankruptcy and been liquidated without the bank recovering their loans, "dead loans," and loans that are two years or more overdue, "doubtful loans," increased by at least half between year-end 1994 and year-end 1997. These data are summarized below. Data reflecting the quality of assets at other major financial institutions, both banks and nonbank financial intermediaries, is more limited. But it appears likely that the quality of assets in these institutions is even lower than that of the four largest state-owned banks. For example, the Agricultural Development Bank, created only in 1994, has grown extremely rapidly and has emerged as China's fifth largest bank, with assets in excess of RMB 710 billion by year-end 1996. But even as its assets have expanded their quality has deteriorated rapidly. The acknowledged share of nonperforming loans surged from 20 percent at year-end 1995 to 26 percent at year-end 1996 and then reached 27 percent by end February 1997.

Asset quality at trust and investment companies, the most important

The Quality of Loans of China's Four Largest State-Owned Banks

	1994	1995	1997
Nonperforming loans	20.3	22	25
of which:			
Overdue	11.3	12	<11.5
Doubtful	7.7	8	>11.5
Dead	1.3	2	2

of the nonbank financial intermediaries, also appears to be worsening.[2] Many of them in the 1990s have reduced their traditional lending and investment activities and increased their exposure to property development and stock brokerage. In addition to shifting into these riskier activities, most have significantly increased their off-balance sheet exposure, mostly in the form of loan guarantees. Guangdong International Trust and Investment Company, for example, by year-end 1997 had extended guarantees equal to almost five times its own capital. Finally, most trust and investment companies have built up huge unhedged foreign exchange exposures. Most of their lending is denominated in foreign currencies. But most of their borrowers have insignificant foreign exchange revenues, meaning that a currency devaluation that eroded the repayment ability of the borrowers would ultimately be reflected in the financial soundness of the trust and investment companies themselves. These problems are acute in part because of inadequate supervision and regulation of trust and investment companies. Although they are nominally regulated by the central bank, the trust and investment companies exist "largely in a regulatory vacuum."[3]

While the quality of the assets of Chinese financial institutions has deteriorated and is now at levels far higher than reported by financial institutions in Thailand and Korea prior to the onset of the Asian financial crisis in 1997, their own capital is extraordinarily low. The capital of the four largest state owned banks, for example, was only 3.1 percent of assets at year-end 1996, down from 13.2 percent at year-end 1985. Moreover, Chinese banks maintain no separate provisions for nonperforming loans.[4]

The lesson of the 1980s, when a large number of countries experienced systemic bank problems, is that financial distress is "likely to become systemic when nonperforming loans, net of provisions, reach 15 percent of total loans." In China, nonperforming loans appear to have reached at least 25 percent, net of provisions. Thus China is well past the point at which a systemic banking crisis might be expected.

A banking crisis in China is most likely to be precipitated when domestic savers lose confidence in the government's implicit guarantee of the value of their deposits in banks. This loss of confidence could be triggered by a growth slowdown that weakened the domestic banking system or by the prospect of a major devaluation in response to a large emerging current account deficit and a sharp fall in inward foreign direct investment. If households in large numbers attempt to withdraw their savings, the insolvency problem of several of China's largest banks could become a liquidity problem. If the central bank were to serve the role of lender of last resort, and supplied funds to banks on a large scale, the resulting increase in the money supply could be highly inflationary. That, in turn, could lead households to reduce their savings in the form of bank deposits, leading to a disruption of the payments system, a collapse of credit, and thus a major recession. A systemic crisis could also lead to a reduction in the long-term household savings rate, imposing a significant constraint on long-term growth.

China has in recent months launched a renewed reform effort that is designed to reduce the risk of macroeconomic instability arising from weaknesses in the financial sector. Since the restoration of the health of the banking and financial system is impossible until there is a change in the fundamental behavior of the most important customers of the banks, this effort is closely tied to fundamental reforms of state-owned firms. The reform effort, which includes a substantial down payment on the required recapitalization of the banking system takes advantage of China's low existing level of domestic debt.

But pushing through fundamental reform of state-owned enterprises is fraught with risks. Rising unemployment, even if it is only transitory, could precipitate massive labor unrest, which could easily derail the real sector restructuring that is so badly needed. Delaying or slowing the current reforms in the short run might mitigate some of the adverse social and political consequences of reform. But its long term consequence would be the loss of the opportunity to create a more efficient system of resource allocation and utilization. Thus delay almost certainly would eventually cause an even lower pace of economic growth, an even slower pace of job creation, and ultimately an even greater challenge to political stability. Thus the leadership may have little alternative but to push its current reform agenda aggressively.

Notes

1. Unless specific sources are cited, all data in this paper are drawn from primary sources cited in Nicholas R. Lardy, *China's Unfinished Economic Revolution* (Washington, D.C.: The Brookings Institution Press, 1998).

2. Moody's Investors Service, *Banking System Outlook: International Trust & Investment Corporations (ITICs) in China, Awkwardly Embracing a New Reality* (New York, April 1998).

3. Moody's Investors Service, *Banking System Outlook*, p. 11.

4. Contrary to international practice, the Chinese count all reserves for nonperforming loans as part of their capital.

6
How Stable Is China? An Economic Perspective

Pieter Bottelier

The Asian financial crisis has raised the level of international anxiety about potential instability in China. How stable is China? Can the country's strong external economic position turn around in a short period of time? Can the society and the political system cope with high and rising urban unemployment? Can agricultural surplus labor be absorbed elsewhere in the economy? Is inflation definitely under control or could it erupt again as happened several times since the beginning of the economic reforms in late 1978? In monitoring the Chinese economy, are we missing or misinterpreting important facts and dynamics as most analysts did in the case of Thailand, Indonesia, Malaysia, the Philippines, and Korea? Since nobody predicted the Asian financial crisis and few "saw it coming," it is prudent to assess China's economic strengths and vulnerabilities.

As a result of turbo-charged growth over the past two decades, China has become the world's seventh largest economy (the second largest on a purchasing power party basis) and the eighth or ninth largest international trader. At current market exchange rates, China's economy is considerably larger, for example, than those of India and Russia combined. Serious instability in China would have global ramifications.

China's Stability Since 1978

The Asian Financial Crisis—China's External Economic Strength

The reason for China's relative invulnerability to contagion following the crisis is the country's strong external economic position:

- Unlike the Asian crisis economies, China had a sizable current account surplus in 1996 and 1997. A smaller surplus is projected for 1998. In other words, China is on balance a net exporter of savings to the rest of the world. The crisis economies (like most developing countries) were significant net users of foreign savings in the precrisis years.
- China's external debt of about $142 billion (about the same level as international foreign exchange reserves) is relatively modest and its maturity composition sound. Short term external debt accounts for only about 25 percent of the total and only a slightly higher share of useable international reserves. Even if short term debt is significantly underestimated, say by a factor of 150 percent as was the case in Korea, China's short term debt to useable reserves ratio—a critical indicator of external vulnerability—is still safe. For comparison, Korea's short term external debt to useable reserves ratio was more than 400 percent before the crisis broke. Most other crisis economies had ratios of between 100–200 percent. The total of all private foreign capital that has flown into China during the past six years (more than $120 billion), came in the form of long-term foreign direct investment (FDI), not as short term bank loans or portfolio investments in local stock exchanges as was more common in the crisis economies.
- China's foreign exchange reserves, at more than $140 billion, are very large relative to imports and other relevant indicators. Moreover, the bulk of reserves is held in relatively liquid form and therefore useable in the event of a crisis. By contrast, only about half of Korea's international reserves were useable when the Asian crisis hit that country in November 1997. The Chinese monetary authorities wish to avoid a further build-up of official reserves. For that reason they have relaxed foreign exchange surrender requirements for exporters, permitted higher levels of foreign investment by Chinese corporations, continued the gradual process of foreign trade liberalization, and raised the amount of foreign exchange that can be purchased by Chinese traveling abroad. (The rate at which new passports are being issued to Chinese citizens for personal travel abroad is now approaching 2 million p.a.)
- Other than British sterling, the Chinese RMB Yuan is the only major currency that appreciated against the U.S. dollar in recent years: about 5 percent in nominal terms since China's devaluation and

successful exchange rate unification of January 1994. Taking account of the substantial cumulative inflation differential between China and her trading partners, effective appreciation of the RMB Yuan between January 1994 and June 1997 was, according to the IMF, about 31 percent, much more than the net effective devaluation for exporters of January 1994, estimated at only 7–8 percent. The fact that China's exports have, until recently, continued to grow so fast in spite of this large effective currency appreciation is remarkable. On the supply side, this can only be explained with reference to the foreign funded (mostly from Hong Kong and Taiwan) export oriented investment boom of the early 1990s, the growing productivity of Chinese export industries, improved marketing and, more recently, decelerating domestic demand which forced many producers to look for outside markets. The post-crisis appearance of small black foreign currency markets in some Chinese cities where the Yuan is traded at a discount, is an aberration due to remaining administrative controls and devaluation fear fed by currency traders in isolated local markets.

- Finally, the fact that China had not (yet) made its currency convertible for capital account transactions, made it virtually impossible for speculators to attack the Chinese currency, even if there had been a reason for trying.

Other Factors Underpinning Current Stability

External economic strength and the awareness of it, are reinforced by a number of political factors that have tended to promote stability and confidence on the part of China's leadership:

- The death of Deng Xiaoping in early 1997 did not lead to internal disturbances or destabilizing political strife, as some foreign observers had expected. On the contrary, it consolidated the collective leadership style that had gradually developed since the early 1990s and enhanced national confidence.
- The restoration of mainland sovereignty over Hong Kong on July 1, 1997 proceeded without the disturbances many had expected. Since that time both sides have observed the Basic Law of 1992. Hong Kong's monetary and fiscal independence have been fully respected. Democratic elections for part of the membership of the

new legislative council were held in May as planned. The Hong Kong economy is currently depressed because of the Asian financial crisis, but there are no indications of politically induced economic problems. It is perhaps ironic that to fight economic recession, the Hong Kong government recently reduced restrictions on private tourism from the mainland.

- Strong reaffirmation of Party commitment to intensify State-owned enterprise (SOE) reform and the development of a modern "rule of law" system, at the opening of the 15th Party Congress in September 1997 and subsequent meetings, provided new impetus and direction to China's incremental marketization process. Broad statements of objective and method by the leadership, have historically played an important role in the evolution of reform policy and institutional development in China.
- The smooth transition in March 1998 from the Li-Peng government to the Zhu Rongji government in accordance with the provisions of the 1982 Constitution was another confidence and stability enhancing event. The new government is younger, more highly educated, and more internationally oriented than the one it replaced.
- The successful visit by President Jiang Zemin to the United States in October 1997, was seen in China as a milestone in the process of gaining international recognition and building a strategic partnership. The return visit to China by President Clinton in June 1998 reinforced that process.
- The fact that China's economy was not subject to sudden crisis or virulent contagion like Thailand, Malaysia, Indonesia, the Philippines, and Korea has reaffirmed the leadership's belief in the merits of the country's gradualist, homegrown approach to reform. China participated in the IMF-led rescue package for Thailand (third largest donor after Japan and the United States) and provided bilateral crisis-related assistance to Indonesia.

The Current Economic Situation and Near Term Outlook

The economic reforms, started at the end of 1978, have brought China the longest period of sustained rapid development with stability in well over a century. The tragic Tiananmen incident did not mark the beginning of renewed instability and decline as many had feared. It led indirectly to an intensification of the development effort and an enormous (uncontrolled) investment boom that refueled inflation. The vast majority of the Chinese population, urban as well as rural, is benefiting from the reforms and supports of the government's economic program. Average disposable per capita income quadrupled and absolute poverty was significantly reduced. Consumer goods and food supplies, in a greater variety and abundance than ever before, are available almost everywhere in urban and rural China. Vastly improved telecommunications and infrastructure have widened and deepened domestic markets to the point where internal competition has become one of the strongest reform driving forces.

The high inflation (economic overheating due to excess investment in real estate and many industries) of 1992/93/94 was successfully overcome with a macro-stabilization program that started mid-1993. As part of this process, China shifted the emphasis in economic control from direct administrative intervention to reliance on indirect instruments of macroeconomic management. A "soft landing" was accomplished in 1996 after wrenching domestic policy adjustments and power shifts. Inflation has dropped out of sight since the middle of 1997. GDP growth gradually dropped from over 14 percent in 1993 to 8.8 percent last year (1997). The successful macro-stabilization program has contributed significantly to China's current stability, and external economic strength. If China had not made the difficult internal policy and institutional adjustments that permitted a "soft landing" in 1996, the Asian financial crisis would probably have dragged the economy down in a much more serious way.

For the last four years, China's GDP growth has gradually slowed. The current Asian financial crisis has accelerated the slowdown; mainly through its depressing effect on exports to Japan and other countries in the region. Growth has now fallen below the magical 8 percent that China's planners consider necessary for successful reform implementation and labor absorption. The leadership is very concerned that growth is falling too far. Evidence of slack domestic demand and excess production capacity is everywhere. Unsold stocks are piling up in many sectors, prices are depressed, and deflation grips the economy. Public sentiment about the economy has become less optimistic. The government's statistics indicate that GDP growth fell to 7.2 percent in the first quarter of 1998 and export growth to 12 percent. However, because of the way in which the State Statistical Bureau measures growth (first quarter 1998 over first quarter 1997, rather than comparing seasonally adjusted numbers for sequential quarters, as is normal practice in most countries) these numbers can be misleading. It is possible, even likely, that GDP growth has already flattened to a lower seasonally adjusted rate. Chinese economic statistics tend to overstate growth in a downturn and vice versa. The most likely outcome for 1998 is somewhere in the range of 6–8 percent. If there is no revival of export demand and if foreign investment falls, as must be anticipated, GDP growth in 1999 could fall below this range.

To protect stability—a key objective of Chinese policy making—the government will undoubtedly do everything possible to reinvigorate the economy. The internal debate is now focused on how this can be accomplished while at the same time improving the quality of growth, which is critical. Is there a conflict between stimulating growth and accelerating market reforms? There could be, but need not be if the interventions are carefully measured and targeted. Strong reliance on broad relaxation of monetary policy that would benefit loss making SOEs as much as sound enterprises, is to be avoided. China is not yet ready for this approach; it would buy a short term growth spurt at the expense of greater financial sector problems in the future. China's half-reformed economy calls for greater selectivity. The government has recently announced that the main emphasis will be on accelerated housing reform and incremental public sector investment in certain types of infrastructure. Housing reform will involve accelerated monetization of housing subsidies and massive privatization of house ownership in urban areas. (Rural housing has traditionally been private.) Housing reform can be a very powerful and efficient tool to stimulate China's economy. It will generate a wave of private demand for housing repairs, remodeling as well as financial reserves such as private mortgage financing.

Given the prospect of a continued strong balance of payments and taking into account the small margin of domestic value added in most exports, there will probably be less emphasis in government policy on promoting foreign demand. The government's firm no-devaluation pledge is most helpful to China's neighbors in crisis, but it is not an act of generosity; it is also in China's interest to keep its exchange rate stable at this juncture. Should the overall balance of payments position deteriorate, a more likely scenario is that China will flexibilize exchange rate policy and allow the "managed float" system, as originally designed for the Shanghai interbank foreign exchange market, to make gradual adjustments. Other instruments to protect exports are available:

- The government can improve the profitability of exporters by elimi-

nating the implied export tax (differential between VAT payable on imported inputs and export rebate);
- The government can relax onerous depreciation rules for income tax purposes and provide other incentives;
- Many light manufacturing enterprises now located at or near the coast can and do relocate to the interior where labor and land cost savings more than compensate for higher transport costs. From an economic perspective, China is not one country, but a collection of countries with substantial differences in factor costs. The theory of shifting comparative advantage between countries at different stages of development, applies equally to China's provinces.

In conclusion, the quality of macroeconomic management in China has significantly improved since the earlier reform period. The external economic situation is very strong. External debt has been managed prudently. The new government is committed to reform and relatively well equipped to face the very tough economic challenges that lie ahead. Although the deceleration in growth has raised concern about stability, there is some room for maneuver and flexible, non-inflationary policy responses to the slowdown or a possible turnaround in the balance of payments. China is studying the causes of the Asian financial crisis to avoid a similar disaster at home. The crisis has added a new sense of urgency to the reform effort, particularly with regard to SOEs and the financial sector. The biggest external threat in the near term future probably lies in the possibility of continuing economic recession in Japan (accounting for almost 20 percent of China's exports in 1996) and/or a deepening of the Asian financial crisis. Yen depreciation helps on the debt side, but makes exporting to Japan harder. The current recession in Hong Kong contributes to the slowdown in China and vice versa. It is unquestionably a source of serious concern. However, the probability of instability in China due to external economic pressures remains low.

Potential Sources of Instability

The most important potential sources of instability in China are internal:

1. Growing unemployment and the lack of adequate social safety nets;
2. Financial sector weakness;
3. Inflation.

Growing Unemployment

China's economic reforms have entered a new and more dramatic phase. It will become increasingly difficult to feel Deng Xiaoping's metaphorical stones as the river is getting deeper. During earlier reform phases, there were relatively few people who lost or did not gain. This has changed. Paradoxically, China's growing unemployment is as much a sign of progress in implementing SOE and other reforms, as it is a major new problem and challenge. Most un- and underemployment in the past was hidden through restrictions or labor mobility and labor redundancy in State enterprises. Agricultural surplus labor, released by strong productivity growth over the past two decades, is now able (and can afford) to travel in search of work and a better life elsewhere. Forced by growing domestic competition and mandated by the fifteenth Party Congress and subsequent reform decisions, numerous medium, small scale, and some larger SOEs are being restructured in a variety of ways: merged, sold, scaled down, or closed. Vast numbers of redundant personnel are being furloughed or laid off in the process.[1]

Transparency of the reforms, including privatization, often leaves much to be desired, but at last, SOE reform is happening on a large scale. Nationwide, it is estimated that some 100,000 out of a total of 300,000 medium and small scale SOEs are available for privatization in a variety of ways. Many have already been sold; many others will be closed for lack of buyers. The process is mostly in the hands of the enterprises themselves or their owners at the township, county, municipal, or provincial level. Some provinces move faster than others. In Liaoning, for example, all SOEs in the province except two steel mills are for sale. About 15 percent of them have been sold. There are too few buyers for the remaining 85 percent. Many SOEs have zero or negative net-worth. The reform process is slower with regard to the 5,000–6,000 large scale SOEs, some of which are the main or only source of employment in smaller towns. The government wishes to retain full ownership and control of about 1,000 strategic SOEs. Accelerated SOE reform should reduce and eventually stop the accumulation of non-performing SOE loans in the banking system.

Slowing domestic demand is adding to the growing open unemployment problem, especially in the Northeast which has a high concentration of large, old, and inefficient SOEs. Total registered urban unemployment presently stands at more than 5 million. To this should be added about half of the 10 million furloughed SOE workers who have not yet found another job. This yields a total number of officially recognized urban unemployed of over 10 million, or about 6.5 percent in the urban labor force,[2] the highest rate since 1949. In addition, there is a large, but unknown number of unemployed migrant workers who do not have a valid urban residence permit needed for unemployment registration. Many of these migrant workers are now voluntarily returning to rural areas—because rural income growth[3] has been stronger in recent years than urban income growth—or are being involuntarily returned home by police. The 6.5 percent urban unemployment rate is a national average. It hides large regional differences. In big cities in the Northeast (e.g., Shenyang), the number is probably closer to 20 percent. The problem is also serious in Wuhan, Chongqing, parts of greater Shanghai, and other cities. By contrast, in young boom towns in the Southeast with few, if any, inefficient SOEs (such as Shenzen) the unemployment rate is very low. Unemployment and social distress have generated protest actions and demonstrations, sometimes of a disruptive and violent nature, in several Chinese cities. If such demonstrations were to assume a political character, they could become dangerous to stability beyond the immediate area where they occur.

In light of the current slowdown in both domestic and export demand growth, intensified SOE reform, the massive recently announced civil service downsizing, continued pressure from rural surplus labor and natural labor force growth (about 15 million p.a.), the open urban unemployment rate must be expected to rise. It could reach 10 percent of the urban labor force in a few years and the average period that laid-off workers are unemployed before they find alternative work, is likely to lengthen. This is precisely what had been feared most about the market economic reforms, why serious SOE reform had been delayed for so long and why the non-State economy was first allowed and later encouraged to grow so quickly. Had more progress been made in the establishment of social safety nets outside the SOE (and work unit) framework, growing urban unemployment would not have been such a serious problem. At the national level, unemployment-induced social distress is not likely to pose a major threat to stability, but in certain regions it is already a serious problem.

Since China's economic reforms cannot be reversed, some provincial governments have opted for accelerated reform, including large scale privatization of SOEs, as the safest and quickest way to overcome the deep structural economic problems that have now become fully apparent and better understood. There is no uniform national pattern or pace of SOE reform in China. The central government is actively promoting the establishment of non-SOE (or work unit-) based social safety nets at the national and regional level through unemployment, health insurance, direct subsidies, pension reform, temporary public work schemes, job retraining programs, and emerging labor market information and placement services. Many programs and lending facilities have been developed by SOEs, work units, and lower level governments to help unemployed workers in starting small private businesses. The scarcity of financial resources, a lack of trained personnel, inadequate institutions, and corrupt practices in some areas are the main obstacles to quick progress. In most parts of China, underdeveloped service sectors such as personal care, marketing, financial services, etc. offer the best hope for labor absorption in an otherwise slowing economy. Serious efforts to facilitate adjustment to new market realities and to reduce the social costs associated with unemployment are being made in most parts of China. Since higher rates of unemployment lie ahead, these efforts need to be intensified. Social tolerances for unemployment and associated hardship are likely to be influenced by public perceptions of the quality and honesty of government, and by expectations. Widespread perceptions of corruption or mismanagement, especially at the local level, will greatly enhance the chances that labor unrest will become politicized and threaten stability.

Financial Sector Weakness and SOE Indebtedness

China's market reforms have yielded impressive economic gains in most areas, but one of the hidden costs of delayed SOE and banking reform has been the gradual deterioration of the asset quality of State commercial banks and the growing indebtedness of SOEs. Much of the SOE debt is non-performing. Consequently, China has a very large internal corporate debt and undercapitalization problem. This has contributed to the financial weakness of State commercial banks and many other financial institutions, and slowed financial sector reform. The problem is probably worse than it was in Korea before the Asian crisis hit that country in November 1997.

In contrast to SOE debt, the State's direct internal debt, at about 10 percent of GDP, is very modest. This factor offers important potential for ultimately writing off bad SOE debt and recapitalizing the State banks. The Asian crisis has heightened the Chinese government's awareness of the dangers of financial sector fragility and excessive corporate indebtedness. If the problem is mismanaged or left unattended, it could eventually lead to a banking crisis and/or high inflation. China's internal debt problem is like a time bomb with a burning fuse of unknown length. It needs to be defused as soon as possible and the way to do it, is to stop the bad debt from growing, followed by a recapitalization of the banks and a write off of uncollectable debt. The government is fully aware of this. Many corporations will also have to be recapitalized. Financial sector problems can be triggered by events outside the banking or SOE sector. The weaker the banks, the more vulnerable they are to unexpected shocks and the greater the need for government or Central Bank intervention in case of trouble. The degree of their vulnerability is, of course, also a function of the availability of alternative options for depositors. The range of options typically widens with reforms, as is also the case in China.

The process of financial sector reform and state bank recapitalization is being accelerated. Many unsound State owned investment corporations and some regional banks that were responsible for overinvestment and subsequent losses in real estate and other sectors, have been closed and their assets disposed of. The government is now considering the establishment of one or more Asset Management Corporations to assist in the disposal of state commercial bank assets associated with non-performing SOE loans. Resolution Trust Company-type operations are beginning to play a role in the massive, highly decentralized SOE reform and privatization task that still lies ahead. One of the most intractable dilemma's facing the Chinese government is that the overriding need to preserve social stability and the very pressing need to restore financial sector health, often lead to different conclusions to the appropriate pace of reform.

The precise degree of undercapitalization of China's four major state commercial banks is essentially unknowable because of the poor state of their accounts. Even after the planned injection of RMB 270 billion (about U.S. $32.5 billion) of new quasi-equity capital by the government, their average risk weighted capital adequacy ratio measured by international standards, remains well below the 8 percent minimum Basle standard. One or more further major equity injections will be needed. A higher rate of bank profitability could also contribute to this process as could an opening to private foreign equity participation in state banks. None of the state commercial banks have so far been audited by international firms; loan classification standards are only now being adjusted to international standards and that will be a time consuming process, because none of China's state banks have adequate provisions or reserves against which to write off bad debt. Because of underprovisioning, their profits tend to be overstated and consequently part of the government's fiscal revenues from banks are based on phantom profits. This is but one illustration of how fiscal problems and banking sector problems in China are interrelated.

In spite of their hugely inflated balance sheets[4], China's large state commercial banks are nonetheless stable, because of the government's implicit guarantee of deposits and most other liabilities. While the Chinese government is stable and its creditworthiness not in doubt, the financial weakness of state commercial banks does not present an acute danger to system stability. A domestic confidence crisis of such magnitude that it would undermine the household deposit base of a large part of the state banking system (accounting for 60 percent of all deposits in China), is hard to imagine. Regional financial problems, however, and the failure of some smaller financial institutions may occur, as happened in recent years. The most serious problem presented by the weakness of most state-owned financial institutions in China, is that this situation may ultimately frustrate reform and modernization efforts and contribute to stagnation. If the reforms get bogged down, the risk of instability in China will greatly increase.

As part of the process of opening domestic markets to foreign competition, it is essential that China open up much further than has been done so far to foreign financial institutions, including commercial banks that take local currency deposits. This has to be a gradual process, but China has tended to err on the cautious side. From a perspective of financial system stability, China can open up the domestic insurance and financial services market quicker than the commercial banking market. More competition in the financial sector is essential for reform and achieving greater efficiency. Unnecessary delays in financial sector reform entails significant risk for China's stability.

SOE Reform at the Micro Level

SOEs in China are no longer so important in terms of their contribution to GDP—they now account for less than 30 percent of industrial output, compared to 80 percent fifteen years ago—but they account for the bulk of state bank assets and the non-performing part of it. The potential for financial system problems grows with the relative size of the non-performing loan portfolio of the banks. Macroeconomic instability is ultimately the reflection of accumulated micro—(or firm level) and banking problems. The Asian financial crisis provides ample evidence of such micro-macro linkages. SOEs in China, like the state banks, have over time become increasingly undercapitalized. The average SOE debt-to-equity-ratio is now probably in the range of 400–700 percent. This ratio used to be much lower in China. For comparison, the average debt/equity ratio for Korean Chaebols before the crisis was about 350 percent. A normal ratio for large U.S. corporations is of the order of 100–150 percent. The debt/equity ratio for manufacturing enterprises in Taiwan, China is an exceptionally low 70 percent. The more highly leveraged, the more vulnerable corporations are to possible increases in interest rates as has been amply demonstrated in the Asian crisis economies, especially Korea. Devaluation and the need for high interest rates to stabilize currencies at their new level has spawned a secondary, this time internal, debt crisis in those countries. A period of high interest rates in China, should the need ever arise, would be extremely problematic for China's unreformed SOEs and state banks. It could destabilize the economy.

The amount of resources that will eventually be required for writing down the bad debt of China's SOEs and recapitalizing the banks and corporations is huge, but probably not beyond China's means, provided the flow of new bad debt is stopped soon. This is the hardest part of the problem. The Chinese government is confident that, in the aggregate, the stock (of bad debt) problem can be solved through a combination of asset sales, privatization, and long-term domestic bond issues that would not create an excessive fiscal burden. Given the large degree of uncertainty with regard to the numbers, it is very difficult to confirm this through objective analysis. China's internal debt problem is in fact even larger and more complicated than indicated above, because of the implicit, but unfunded pension debt of the State and its enterprises. This has become an issue, because China has decided to reform the pension system in the direction of funded individual accounts which means that in the future, payroll deductions for pensions are no longer available to fund current pension obligations through the transfer payment system.

Ultimately, successful, non-inflationary SOE and banking sector reform plus recapitalization as well as pension reform, will to a large extent depend on very substantial improvements in fiscal revenues and the budget system. None of the aggregate internal problems can or have to be solved overnight. If there is rapid progress at the micro level through privatization, firm level efficiency improvements, closure of bad firms, manpower training, etc., the time bomb can still be diffused. However pressing the financial sector and SOE problems, China has no option but to continue pursuing a more or less gradual approach to reform. There is no room for a "big-bang" approach that would try to solve all major structural economic and financial problems simultaneously. It makes no sense to write off the accumulated stock of bad SOE debt until the flow of new bad debt has stopped. Otherwise, the expectation of and need for new capital write-offs will inevitably develop, undermining credibility of the government and integrity of the financial system. Even if the government wanted to pursue a comprehensive once-and-for-all solution to the SOE bad debt problem, there wouldn't be a sufficiently reliable data base on which to make firm level decisions. In the meantime, the financial weakness of China's state banks remains a potential threat to stability, because of the vulnerability to shock that are inherent to weakness.

Inflation

It may seem strange to raise inflation as an issue at this time, as the problem does not appear to be on the horizon. Yet, the half-reformed status of China's economy, the current economic slowdown, and the huge internal debt balloon, could rekindle inflation if too much liquidity is injected into the system in an effort to stimulate the economy or solve other problems. Fortunately, the fear of inflation and the damage it can do to the economy and social stability, is deeply ingrained in China's leadership. Their ability to manage excess demand—in the past mostly due to excess investment—has greatly improved. The successful macrostabilization program that was started in mid-1993 is a source of pride. Noone would consciously risk monetary stability. But the dilemmas and policy conflicts are very complex and intense. Although the lessons of the past appear to have been learned well, policy mistakes can be made and inflation could reappear, also for other reasons.

Macroeconomic management mistakes that could lead to inflation appear less likely at this stage than the possibility of certain micro level developments that could have the same effect. The stock of money supply in China (M2) has become very large in relation to GDP (well over

100 percent). The velocity of money circulation has been steadily declining over the years. This has contributed to inflation reduction and large earnings by the Central Bank in the form of seignorage. The low and declining velocity of circulation is a reflection of public confidence in continued stability, a high preference for liquid assets and low efficiency of payment systems. None of these factors are likely to be subject to sudden, massive change, but there is nothing permanent about them either. Should there be an increase in velocity, due for example to confidence loss, inflation could reemerge rather quickly as people invest liquid financial assets in goods, houses, or foreign exchange. This is what happened in 1988/89. The high inflation of that period is one of the factors that contributed to popular support for political demonstrations in Beijing and other cities. Ultimately, as payment systems modernize and alternatives to liquid financial assets in local currency become more easily available, the ratio of money supply to GDP will come down, but it is essential for stability that this process be gradual.

A change in savings behavior is another possible micro level source of renewed inflationary pressure. The Chinese financial system depends on exceptionally large private household savings and current account deposits (about 60 percent of total deposits) to keep it afloat. A large part of these savings is invested by the banks in SOE loans that are nonrecoverable, but the government's implicit deposit guarantee protects confidence and system stability. However, a reduction in the private savings rate (which has been extremely high over many years) would weaken the deposit base of state banks and put pressure on them to accelerate debt write offs and/or restrict new lending. Under those circumstances, Central Bank intervention to avoid unwanted bankruptcies and to protect growth, may become hard to resist. Such intervention, if it occurs on a large scale could be inflationary.

Finally, there is, of course the possibility of large agricultural production shortfalls due to natural disasters or big policy mistakes. Harvests have been excellent in the last three years and food supplies are plentiful. Grain stocks are at a historical high and domestic grain prices fell by over 10 percent during the past twelve months. (This explains all or most of the recent drop in the retail price index.) A bad grain harvest in 1998 could probably be met from existing stocks, but two bad agricultural years in a row, could generate food price-led inflation, because China cannot import grain beyond a certain level, even if international supplies were available. China's reforms still have a long way to go and the possibility of renewed inflation due to either macro- or micro-level factors, cannot be ruled out.

Notes

1. Normally, redundant workers employed in reforming SOEs are first placed on extended furlough with retention of their homes and minimal financial support. Many find other work with or without the help of State sponsored retraining and job search programs within twelve months.

2. Institute of Economics, China Academy for Social Sciences.

3. In rural areas that depend mainly on grain farming, incomes have stagnated or fallen in recent years because of sharp grain price drops induced by excess supply. Most non-grain agricultural production (accounting for about half of agriculture), however, has sustained rapid income growth in many rural areas.

4. The amount of non-performing loans (NPL) appearing as assets on the balance sheet of State commercial banks is estimated at about 25 percent of the total and an even higher percentage of GDP. Not all NPLs, however, are non-performing because the debtor is unable to pay. There are a number of circumstances under which debtors and creditors have shared interest in keeping loans in the non-performing category and to capitalize interest which under current rules (that are to be changed) is legal for up to two years.

7
The Potential for Urban Unrest: Will the Fencers Stay on the Pisté?*

Dorothy J. Solinger

Urban unrest is plentiful in China today, even surging, according to many reports. So there is no question to be posed about the "potential" for urban unrest. But is this the same thing as asking if China's cities are likely to become truly unstable? I would maintain that it is not. Indeed, it is possible to adopt a perspective according to which the multifold state-worker confrontations that crop up frequently in the municipalities—encounters which range very widely in type, scope, and content—are almost stylized, scripted, even poised in a stasis.

The big enigma, then, is not so much whether there *will be* "unrest"—a concept that, after all, covers a vast array of motions, contains a wealth of meanings. Instead, the puzzle is really about:

- Whether the disturbances currently occurring will escalate in the extent of upheaval they occasion;
- Whether they will extend in scale, expand in numbers, and increase in degree of daring, scope, and duration;
- Will today (and yesterday's) sporadic disorder, not yet of a really explosive or an all-inclusive sort, graduate and erupt into steady turmoil, replete with constant riots, violence, and serious destruction?;
- What are the factors and the circumstances that could bring China to such a pass?

*In fencing, the pisté is the playing field, a long, narrow strip within the bounds of which players must remain, moving only forward and backward along it.

This chapter will focus on the dynamics that attend the present context, and use the result of the analysis to extrapolate from the immediate scene to possible later developments. For simplicity's sake, as well as to sharpen the assessment, I will cast the analysis in terms of a stark, and very interactive opposition between two symbolic, collective parties, "the state" and "the workers." My investigation of the dynamics will include:

- A look at the chief concerns of both parties,
- Their customary behavioral inclinations,
- The degree of organization each possesses, and
- Most importantly, the nature of what I will call the "weapons" that each side is able to wield and bring to bear in its engagement with the other.
- I then illustrate this interactive dynamic by descriptions of conflicts common in Chinese cities over the past decade[1] and their resolutions (or lack thereof).
- Next I turn to another critical element in the picture: the context, or more precisely several contexts, in which protest has taken place in recent years in China. During the past decade-plus, the targets of protest and the claims and demands have not varied greatly, but neither have they been invariant.
- My principal claim in considering dynamics and context is that commotion caused by the workers cannot be viewed in isolation: rather, it is a function of *the interaction of the workers with the state*; it is also a function of *a shifting and uncertain larger context.*
- Finally, in order to evaluate the potential for far more ominous commotion in the near term, I suggest how the *dynamics* I will specify—dynamics that have preserved a relative stasis up till now—might break down; I do so by speculating about what kind of *contextual elements* might cause them to do so.

I should note here that, hypothetically, there could be a turn for the better as much as a turn for the worse in coming years. But that would appear to hinge on such total transformation of the parameters of action and such fundamental switches in the disposition of the agents and their respective resources that it becomes impossible to use the contours of the present to conjecture about the future. And projection from the known is the only kind that I would venture to advance.

An Interactive Dynamic

As just noted, the most important point about worker unrest is its essentially interactive nature. Workers react, both in relation to the treatment they receive from their own bosses and local officials, and also to state policies and the overall politico-economic context in which they find themselves. Thus, since workers do not create chaos in a vacuum, we need to identify the type of dynamic in which they participate.

It is illuminating to think of the bond between workers and the state in this time of strain as one between players in a game of fencing. Like the interchange between dissatisfied workers and the wary state, fencing entails constant, intense, and perennial vigilance. One cannot make a move without watching one's adversary; a thrust is always calculated to catch one's contender off balance. One must always expose only the minimum of one's body, and take minute steps with quick motions to shield oneself to the maximum without betraying one's intent. The element of surprise is critical.[2]

Fencers can choose to duel with one of three forms of weapon—foil, epee, or saber, in ascending order of power and destructiveness. In fencing, however, the two opponents each always employs the same weapon in any one match, and each party can count on the other to abide by the particular rules that go with that weapon; this is by no means the case in this Chinese contest.

- The foil is a light, flexible thrusting weapon, designed to score with its point on a very specific target area. In order to score, or touch, in foil fencing, the fencer must first gain priority, or right of way, over his opponent. Once established, the opponent is totally on the defensive, and cannot think about attacking until he somehow blocks or parries your threat.[3]
- The epee is a heavier tool with a stiffer blade. Using the epee, the "entire body is a valid target area." Also, "Unlike foil, you don't need priority to score. This means scoring comes fast and furious. Even simultaneously."[4]
- With the third implement, the saber, "you can score by cutting as well as thrusting [so that] saber fencing has larger, more dramatic movements than foil or epee..., and head cuts are a big part of this sport." Indeed, "cutting accounts for most of the scoring in saber."[5]

In fencing the duelers share one sole objective: to make points by touching the other. In worker-state encounters the goal of each side is similar one to the other, but not identical.

- The state (or, more properly, those who run it) prizes stability, certainty for the regime, and for the present form of governing;
- Protesting workers, however, want security just for themselves, certainty of their own employment, wages, and the wherewithal for subsistence on an individual (or familial) plane;
- Given what could be categorized as an implicit agreement on both sides on the value of security—if of different sorts—peace, at least at the macro level, has yet to be obtained.

Even if one prefers not to grant this image of tacit consensus, we could still concede that since each party's aim is a form of ensured sustenance, a condition it ultimately depends upon the other to provide, neither has yet been prone to tip the scales irrevocably. Each party plays this fencing game in an effort to ensure the version of security it values. Of course, in attempting to do so, each does indeed need to try to "touch" the other; in urban unrest the players do so in a variety of ways and using disparate arms.

Quite unlike fencing, however, beyond their shared concern with security what has locked the two players into place in this state of stasis is not any formal (or even informal) "rules of the game." Instead, three other factors sustain the contest in its present form:

- An implicit agreement—and the ability—of each side up until now to draw on a fixed battery of *instruments* (including the resources each commands as one of these);
- The quality and degree of *organization* upon which each side can draw and the gross imbalance between the sides in this regard; and
- The dominant *behavioral inclinations* of the members of each camp.

Even though the aim (and, by stretching things) even the means ("touching") could in a very general sense be said to be parallel for the players in Chinese cities, the implements they each have at their disposal for achieving their aim are far from commensurate. The regime (or the central government, the state) has an impressive range of instruments and contrivances (what could be called resources), including:

- A large measure of *ideological control* over the media and publications;
- A relatively compliant cadre of *personnel and agencies*, hierarchically arrayed to respond to its commands;
- Enough control over *material resources and economic policy* to govern interest rates, disburse emergency relief funds, and even shift macroeconomic strategy; and,
- Far from least of all, *coercive authority* over repressive force, in the form of police and security personnel throughout the country.

We might think of this set of endowments as a graduated package of weapons, moving from foil (in the ideological realm) to epee, more powerful but not likely to wound (in the material realm), to saber, where genuine physical prowess comes into play, entailing intimidation, dispersing workers, injuries, deaths,[6] and detention, sometimes briefly but sometimes for labor reeducation lasting three years or more.

The workers, however, are not without devices. To utilize a parallel framework:

- Workers' foil includes mild and not-so-mild forms of simple harassment, or, as the foil always does, of gaining—or trying to gain—right of way (visits to government offices, demonstrations and marches in—and blocking—the streets, letters of complaint to officials, sit-ins in front of bureaucratic buildings, petitions, and protest rallies, as well as what is called "everyday noncompliance,"[7] such as slow-downs, work evasion, and absenteeism).
- Moving up to epee, whose target is larger, workers go on strike, sometimes in very large numbers;[8] labor activists had also begun to fashion what Human Rights Watch Hong Kong director Robin Munro (perhaps over-optimistically) termed "a formidable network" by early 1994.[9]
- And workers too have a saber, if a generally less fearsome one so far, as compared with the ones in the hands of the state: groups of enraged laborers have sabotaged factory equipment, assaulted offices, committed arson against state property, and detained, attacked, and even killed managers and other bosses. According to one report, in 1993 there were 2,500 (recorded, publicized) cases in which workers became violent, besieging plants, setting fire to facilities, engaging in strikes or detaining their bosses.[10]

Up through mid-1998, workers as a group could sometimes be said to be reasonably endowed for meeting the prowess of the state head-on on the spot and in the moment. But because of the imbalance in organizational capabilities between them and the state (at whatever level), for the most part their weapons have usually tended to be wielded by smallish groups and for only brief periods. As Anita Chan has noted in speaking of workers in foreign firms, where recruits are often easily cowed, only temporarily employed, ignorant of their rights, and, within a given plant, hailing from multiple rural areas, "Almost all of the industrial actions in the FIEs are unorganized, spontaneous wildcat strikes by desperate workers at their wits' end."[11]

In the state firms, problems of organizing large-scale collective action are present as well. The relative uniformity within the plant (if we discount the division into activists and ordinary workers that Andrew Walder has documented) of the pre-reform days has increasingly been replaced by fragmentation, in accord with gender, native place, and market capacity of the workers.[12] Workers' disparate positions, both within and among firms dispose them to react differentially to market reforms and state withdrawal.[13] Cases of whole firm—and, even more difficult to achieve, multi-firm—protests are still relatively rare.

Not only that, but there also appears to be regional variation in the incidence of unrest, with the bulk of it occurring in the impoverished Northeast and in several inland provinces,[14] where unemployment is highest, and less along the coast (with the exception of areas where foreign-invested firms are situated). This comparative disorganization has meant that, outraged as any contingent of laborers might be, their challenges—whether with foil, epee, or saber—tend to be blunted by their geographical and temporal boundedness,[15] certainly in relation to the organizational clout of the state. Moreover, one crucial component of the clout of the state in maintaining this impotent lack of organization among labor is its deliberate drive to date to cut down or keep on the lam any nonofficial workers' unions, by means of its oppressive regulations, ubiquitous surveillance, and its security personnel's arbitrary arrests.

So the superior organizational weight of the state has thus far been able to forestall or to overcome whatever tool the workers may ply, usually by using its epee or its saber—that is, by employee buyoffs and enterprise bailouts or by force.[16] This is the case not only because of the multifaceted package of weapons—ideological, personnel, material, and coercive—that it commands. It is also because the central state and local governments are in accord on the overriding value of stability—though some localities and factories and their officials have appealed to the center for relief funds while central leaders such as Zhu Rongji have tried to get provincial and municipal governments to foot the wage bills;[17] and though local police often act on their own authority.

Possibly there are disagreements among top leaders as to just how to appease disgruntled workers. For instance, a Hong Kong commentator disclosed in spring 1994 that Jiang Zemin, Li Peng, and Qiao Shi were ready to suspend or even halt reform policies where stability was seriously affected;[18] two years later another claimed that Li Peng, Jiang Zemin, and Hu Jintao were prepared to slow down market reforms to ensure the standard of living of the working class.[19] These reports seem to suggest that one key central politician, Zhu Rongji, had other tactics in mind for pacifying the proletariat.[20] But clearly these leaders all agree that peace among the workforce is a critical goal.

Thus, the high priority of this shared objective, both for the bureaucrats of the state at every echelon and for their industrial deputies in the plants, means that they are prepared to act in accord and back each other up—and surely they collectively, up until now, have had the means to do so. In short, working together as a fairly unified force on at least this one issue, the governors of this sometimes "fragmented authoritarian state" (to use the formulation of Kenneth Lieberthal and D. Michael Lampton)[21] can solidify their efforts.

In addition to the driving concern of each side for security, their respective baggages of weaponry, and their differential organizational attributes, the behavioral inclinations of both parties keep the game going as it has been. For many of the workers, there remains a strong residue of stubborn faith that the state, sometimes even the firm, will take care of them paternally as it always has. They appear to have confidence that their appeals are rightfully grounded; in addition, their expectations are of entitlements, and their loyalties have not been totally shattered. As Ching Kwan Lee has quite insightfully observed,

> workers who are most critical of market socialism are also those most dependent on the Chinese state to take care of them and therefore least likely to translate their collective experience of state-led betrayal into collective action.[22]

Marc Blecher's 1997 research in Tianjin uncovered a pattern of four responses to economic retrenchment among workers, none of which was oppositional. Indeed, many of the workers assumed either that "socialism" would protect them in the end or that their own organizational capacities were too weak to contend with the state.[23] Neither of these researchers has interviewed the really embittered. But even among these people, there seems to be a presumption that protesting for such basic needs as simply "food" will attract the sympathy and then the supplies from the leadership that they require.[24]

On the side of the state, though many of the firms themselves no longer have the wherewithal to fulfil the paternalistic obligations of the past, the regime is poised to force them to do so, wherewithal or not. For instance, there are rulings at both central and local levels mandating that the enterprises must take responsibility for training, welfare, and redeployment when possible when workers are dismissed.[25] Behavioral inclinations, then, whether by long-ingrained instinct or by dint of state dictate, have lingered around in the face of institutional change, taming somewhat the ferocity of response on both sides of the playing field (or piste, in fencing language). Thus,

- Shared concerns and objectives (in a manner of speaking);
- Residual behavioral inclinations on both sides;
- An organizational imbalance that cannot be righted under current conditions; and
- A set of unmatched, but still reasonably effective weapons in the hands of the two parties

have all contributed to the ongoing playing-out of a relatively static game of fencing—except that the rules are volatile, the tools used more or less arbitrarily. A look at a few typical strikes will bear out my insistence that, regardless of these two notable infractions of the fundamental regulations of fencing proper, we are nonetheless dealing with a very closed and interactive process.

Strikes. An article in the Spring 1998 issue of *China Rights Forum* by Judy M. Chen briefly describes three incidents:

- The first, in which 400 Hefei textile workers sat in (using their foil), to protest job loss, came to a peaceful conclusion when government officials met with the workers and agreed to help;
- In the second, when workers at Beijing's 3501 Military Uniform

Factory complained about being dismissed with 10,800 yuan in severance pay but no monthly stipend or medical insurance, more than a dozen rounds of fruitless negotiation with officials led them to attempt to hold a march on a main road (also using a foil), but they were denied the necessary permit;

- In the third, a demonstration in Zigong, Szechuan was terminated with at least ten protesters injured and twenty others arrested.[26]

The author supplies so few details that it is impossible to draw conclusions as to why the authorities responded the first time with their foil (in my categorization), the second by parrying with their epee, and the third with sabers. One clue to the blatant denial in the second case is that the protest was led by Zhu Rui, a veteran of the 1979 Democracy Wall Movement, and it is quite likely that the authorities were consequently loath to provide any opening for a potentially politically charged display of opposition. But in these examples we can observe the gamut of regime response, as well as a range of worker stances.

- In another case already alluded to above, when Shenyang staff and workers threatened to call a city-wide strike—clearly an epee advance ("the entire body is a valid target area")—as it spread to some forty enterprises and factories, the State Council told the provincial leader who begged for its guidance to hurry home from the NPC meeting he was attending in order to handle the emergency.
- In still another, when a coal mine in Fushun, Liaoning intended to cut 20,000 miners, the miners responded with a dozen slowdown actions and petitions. The upshot was that the provincial government felt compelled to announce a pledge that not one single worker would lose his/her job and that there would be no default in the payment of wages, bonuses, or allowances.[27]
- In yet other instances, workers in Beijing and Wuhan were permitted to march in small lanes out of the sight of city residents; at other times workers were paid all their outstanding wages with emergency funds donated by the central government.[28]

Several stories speak of one side or the other giving in in the face of uncompromising intransigence by the other. Some tell of workers only being placated when they were promised emergency funds issued from the higher levels.[29] By the same token, only when over 100 miners repeatedly took to the streets, pressing for the immediate disbursal in time for New Year's of wages delayed for four months did mine officials come up with at least two months of pay. As the commentator telling the story in the paper concluded:

> Workers used to demonstrate just once to get the government to pay attention and the problem was more or less resolved. They predict now that the use of demonstrations to settle problems will happen more and more.[30]

Other cases of this sort occurred on a larger scale, as when, reportedly, central leaders backed off on major reform programs earlier in the decade when worker resistance proved too threatening. In one case the labor contract system was said to have been abandoned in 1991 in response to stiff defiance; in another, plans to modernize state enterprises by converting them into stock companies were dropped in 1994.[31]

None of this is to deny that coercion plays a role: sometimes this is clearly because saber is met with saber. For example, when rampaging construction workers wrecked a Party headquarters on the outskirts of Shenzhen in 1995, they were answered with machine-gun fire from the local police and ten people died in the melee.[32] But in other instances, peaceful protests (foils) have brought out the security forces; in yet others what began ominously did not necessarily end up that way. When workers rallied over the issue of staff reduction in 1992 at the Seagull Watch Factory in Tianjin, police, including members of the paramilitary People's Armed Police, were summoned to restore order.[33]

And in Chongqing in 1993, the city government sent out the riot police when retirees marched for their pensions for five days. In the end, however, despite the display of force, the authorities agreed to restore pensions, to find new jobs for those over 35, and to provide training, wages, and allowances for those below that age.[34]

There are probably hidden reasons that explain these seemingly anomalous situations when a weapon used on one side is countered with one much more powerful on the other. The safest conclusion is simply that each party is equipped with its own weapons and styles, and that responses from the state are very likely reactions not to reality but to fear and perceptions, however exaggerated or unfair. But the stories above do indicate the deep interconnectedness between worker moves and official initiatives and responses. So far both sides seem inclined to preserve this apparently unpredictable but ultimately relatively stable pattern.

A Transformation from Scripts to Turmoil? Workers have made their grievances known in their various ways for at least a dozen years by now. Over the years the sources of their grievances in the state sector have ranged from:

- the early moves to dissolve the socialist world of secure jobs and entitlements and growing inequality in the late 1980s;
- to reductions in state investment and large-scale shutdowns of projects in the early 1990s;
- to more job losses and credit cutbacks, followed by inflation and frozen salaries for labor in the midst of increasingly more corrupt behavior of officialdom and management in the mid-1990s; and finally
- to arbitrary dismissals, elimination of benefits, and long unpaid wages and pension allowances in the late 1990s.

In the foreign-invested sector, the issues have consistently been

- poor treatment and harassment;
- long hours;
- low wages; and
- miserable, unhygienic, and unsafe working and living conditions.[35]

And yet despite this ongoing set of assaults on workers' lives and livelihoods, and regardless of the discontent workers clearly experienced in response to them, the game of fencing—of one side initiating and the other reacting to limit the fall-out—has gone on unabated. In short, it seems that overall so far the context for the fencing match has been one in which the externalities of economic reform have been manageable—even if sometimes very unpleasant—for both sides.

To draw upon the dynamic laid out above, this stylized stasis is the result of unchanged inclinations and a more or less constant level of organizational strength among the workforce and the political elite, respectively. It is also the outcome of a continuing ability to employ a constant battery of weapons on both sides.

- First, the use of *material payoffs* has been constant:
- In 1994, for instance, Beijing earmarked over 3 billion yuan for wages owed in order to prevent strikes and demonstrations, even as the state's budget deficit mounted.[36]
- Similarly, emergency funding was dished out over New Year's in

1996, when ministers and local governments were authorized to provide payouts, especially if there were demands or other threats to stability, again during a time of tight monetary policy.[37]

- Following this pattern Beijing pledged more resources for social welfare in the Ninth Five Year Plan, which began in 1996, and established a Social Security component within the Ministry of Labor in 1998, while planning to create a central fund to assist laid-off workers, and to expand the urban social insurance system.
- At the same time, *coercive controls* are still as available as ever. Just as the Ministry of Public Security set up a patrol police force in the cities for the first time at the end of 1993,[38] so today the Beijing City People's Armed Police (PAP) and the Beijing Garrison of the PLA were given orders to cancel leaves and enter a state of readiness in case of social disturbances around the time of the June 4th anniversary.[39]
- Nor have *ideological tools* been abandoned, despite that one might question their efficacy. As the Communist Party's Central Propaganda Department organized work conferences on ideological education for workers four years ago, so this spring central leaders beefed up their supervision and control over the press and publications agencies.[40]
- The appeal to *personnel management* persists as well, with Zhu Rongji urging the top leaders at all levels of the Party and government personally to grasp the work of reemployment of laid-off workers and to delegate capable people to oversee this work early in 1998.[41]

All of this appears to suggest the likelihood of simply more of the same, regardless of minor changes in policy and context, at least for the near term: it implies that the state is yet equipped with the weapons that kept the game in place to date.

And yet, there may be factors afloat that will alter the context very significantly, forcing the players off the piste. For one thing, official policy took a radical turn last fall: as a result, 12 million workers lost their jobs in 1997 and another 11 million are expected to become laid off or fired outright in 1998.[42] "The volume and duration of aid" required to meet the needs of these people, Judy Chen points out, "far outweighs the funding available." She also notes that the State Statistical Bureau has reported that only half the suspended workers have received the stipends promised them.[43] Thus, it looks possible that at least two of the critical factors supporting the stasis could change: workers' inclinations of loyalty and the state's ability to control the situation through the use of one of its most potent weapons, its epee or material resources.

But given the similarities in kind (if not always in degree) over more than a decade in the inclinations, instruments, and organization of the workers and the state, even in what have been tough times already, it would seem that a force from outside the game would have to appear to upset the balance altogether. This would most likely derive from the external economy—in the form of extreme competition from Southeast Asia and/or a severe decline in foreign investment in China, both of which have already begun to reduce the country's growth rate to some extent. Were such developments to accelerate and escalate, they could change the terms of the game in a way that might drive the players off the piste.

For such eventualities could more drastically undermine the material resources the regime can bring to bear to buy off and placate the workforce than has any other circumstance to date; this in turn could greatly undermine the majority of workers' willingness to believe in the state's ability to succor them. But even in such a case, the coercive force of the state would be pitted against the dwindling ability of workers to organize against it. In the absence of a truly catastrophic meltdown, one which severely eviscerated the state's resources and the workers' inclination to carry on with the duel in a scripted form, the game of fencing seems apt to be sustained.

Notes

The author thanks Sue Anderson, Barbara Bernstein, Danching Ruan, and Wang Feng and his father for discussing this topic with her.

1. As far back as 1986, work stoppages and strikes had already appeared among temporary workers in the Shenzhen Special Economic Zone, home of a multitude of foreign-funded firms (see *Foreign Broadcast Information Service* (hereafter *FBIS*), August 23, 1988, 41, from Beijing Domestic Service, August 19, 1988). In 1988, "strikes and slowdowns" were reported to be "breaking out as the government moves to dismantle the socialist system of life-time employment" (*FBIS*, September 6, 1988, 36). A sensational exposure, purportedly drawn from a secret State Council report, appeared in the Hong Kong periodical *Zheng Ming* in early 1994, asserting that more than 6,300 "illegal strikes" and 210 riots had occurred in China just in the year 1993 (see *Zheng Ming* [Contend] (hereafter *ZM*) 198, 21, in *FBIS*, March 31, 1994, 28).

2. Comments from Sue Anderson, who once fenced, May 25, 1998, Irvine.

3. Doug Werner, *Fencer's Start-Up: A Beginner's Guide to Traditional & Sport Fencing* (San Diego: Tracks Publishing, 1997), 45–46.

4. Ibid., 73–74

5. Ibid., 87–88.

6. According to *FBIS*, April 19, 1996, 29, a State Council report cited in *Eastern Express* of the same date alleged that in 1995 there were eighty-five incidents in which 490 persons were injured or killed (though it fails to explain whether state agents or workers were the causes of the casualties).

7. See Ching Kwan Lee, "The Labor Politics of Market Socialism: Collective Inaction and Class Experiences Among State Workers in Guangzhou," *Modern China* 24, 1 (1998): 3–33.

8. For instance, *FBIS* April 14, 1994, twenty-eight reports that a March 1994 strike in Shenyang spread to forty enterprises and factories; its April 19, 1996 edition, on p. 29, claimed that in 1995 there were eleven incidents nationwide involving 10,000 workers each. *Summary of World Broadcasts* (hereafter *SWB*) FE/3217, G/11 (from Xinhua April 30, 1998) claimed that in 1997 the total number of labour disputes topped 71,000, more than double the figure in 1995. It is important to point out, however, that, according to the *Hong Kong Standard* (in *FBIS*, September 27, 1994, 62), only a fifth of the disputes that occur are officially recorded. Anita Chan, in "Labor Relations in Foreign-Funded Ventures, Chinese Trade Unions and the Prospects for Collective Bargaining," in Greg O'Leary, ed., *Adjusting to Capitalism: Chinese Workers and the State* (Armonk, N.Y.: M.E. Sharpe, 1998), 145, n. 27 also makes the point that, "It is extremely difficult to know the exact number of labor disputes in China because the statistical figures released are not standardized."

9. *FBIS*, March 28, 1994, 67. The issue of *FBIS* three days later reported that Liu Nianchun's autonomous workers league "fell apart amid internal bickering almost as soon as it was announced" (from *Eastern Express*, March 31, 1994, 9).

10. *FBIS*, June 2, 1994, 22 (from *Tangtai* [Contemporary Times] 38, May 15, 1994, 20–22).

11. Chan, *op. cit.*, 142.

12. Ching Kwan Lee, "Disorganized Despotism: Transition From Neo-Traditionalism in Guangzhou Factories." Presented at the 50th Annual Meeting of the Association for Asian Studies, 26–29 March 1998, Washington, D.C. [revised version], 3, 29.

13. See Lee, "The Labor Politics."

14. Lee, "Disorganized Despotism," 30.

15. *FBIS*, December 29, 1995, 17 (from *South China Morning Post* (hereafter *SCMP*), December 28, 1995, 7) states that (according to Wily Wo-Lap Lam), "Most of the protests lasted no more than a few days."

16. Other methods exist, too, such as arbitration committees, which reportedly heard 12,348 disputes in 1993 and settled 92 percent of them (*FBIS*, May 2, 1994, 37; also, *FBIS*, January 25, 1996, 10); providing unemployment insurance, vocational training and placement services for the unemployed; barring particular occupations to competing migrant peasant labor; preferential treatment in taxes and loans for jobless workers who begin their own businesses; and writing new laws that promise redress.

17. On Zhu's efforts, see Willy Wo-Lap Lam, *SCMP*, December 7, 1994, 1, 10, reprinted in *FBIS*, December 7, 1994, 43. There are many cases of localities appealing for funds from above.

18. Cheng Yuen, "Strike Movements Occur Frequently on Mainland," *ZM* 198, April 1, 1994, 30–31, in *FBIS*, April 14, 1994, 27.

19. Willy Wo-Lap Lam, *SCMP*, February 9, 1996, 9, reprinted in *FBIS*, same date, 34.

20. For instance, in 1994 he approved the allocation of 500 million yuan as a relief fund for jobless workers. See *FBIS*, June 2, 1994, 22.

21. Kenneth G. Lieberthal and David M. Lampton, eds., *Bureaucracy, Politics and Decision Making in Post-Mao China* (Berkeley: University of California Press, 1992).

22. Lee, "The Labor Politics," 15–16.

23. Marc Blecher, "What are Chinese Workers Thinking?" Paper presented at the panel on "China's New Factory Regime (Part 1)," Association for Asian Studies Annual Meeting, March 28, 1998, Washington, D.C., 9, 10, 20.

24. Workers in Heilongjiang coal mines and elsewhere in 1994 said they were not demanding liberty and democracy but only "work, food, and money" (Zhu Chaolai, "Workers in Unrest," China Focus 2, 6 (1994), 4) and Lu Yu-shan, CPC Guards Against Mass Disturbances, *Tangtai* 38 (May 15, 1994, 20–22), in *FBIS*, June 2, 1994, 22; and into 1995 workers went to the streets in up to ten provinces demanding "food to eat" (*Shijie Ribao* [World Journal]) (hereafter *SJRB*), May 8, 1995.

25. In *SWB* FE/3228, G/4 (May 16, 1998), Jiang Zemin is quoted as saying that enterprises must set up reemployment service centers to ensure workers' living standards, to train them, and to help them find new jobs. And according to Lee, "Disorganized Despotism," 16, Guangzhou officials wrote up regulations limiting managers' autonomy to dismiss labor and requiring them to rehire their own laid-off staff when they can.

26. Judy M. Chen, "A Ricebowl in Pieces: The Unemployment Crisis Bites," *China Rights Forum* (Spring 1998): 38–39.

27. *FBIS*, April 14, 1994, 28.

28. *FBIS*, September 28, 1994, 30 (from Hong Kong *Lien Ho Pao* [United Daily]) and *SJRB*, January 19, 1998.

29. For instance, *FBIS*, December 7, 1994, 43 (from *SCMP* of the same day). *SJRB*, February 11, 1998 tells of a recent case of this sort, in which several 100 laid-off and retired workers in Wuhan sitting in at the factory gate demanding back wages and pensions soon expanded to 3,000, at which point the company immediately posted an urgent notice, agreeing to allow the demonstrators to go to the bank to collect their wages.

30. *SJRB*, January 16, 1998.

31. *FBIS*, May 15, 1991, 21 (from Agence France Presse, interview with then-Labor Minister Ruan Chongwu) and *FBIS*, March 3, 1994, 31 (from *SCMP*, March 2, 1994).

32. Peter Stein, "China Learns to Like Migrant Workers," *Wall Street Journal*, December 12, 1995, A16.

33. *FBIS*, May 29, 1992, 11, from *SCMP*, May 28, 1992.

34. *FBIS*, April 6, 1993, 66 (from *ZM* 186, 37).

35. See my "The Chinese Work Unit and Transient Labor in the Transition from

Socialism," *Modern China* 21, 2 (1995), 155–83.

36. *FBIS*, March 3, 1994, 31 (from *SCMP*, March 2, 1994).
37. *FBIS*, February 9, 1996, 34 (from *SCMP*, same date).
38. *FBIS*, March 3, 1994, 31.
39. *SWB* FE/3234, G/4 (May 23, 1998).
40. *FBIS,* June 2, 1994, 22.
41. *SJRB*, February 16, 1998.
42. Chen, *op. cit.*, 38.
43. Ibid., 39. This may not be as portentous as it sounds, since even if only one fifth of the incidents are reported (see note 8 above), it is still highly unlikely that anywhere near half the workers will demonstrate under present circumstances. For instance, in 1991, another very tense time for the workforce, one reporter noted that the 37,450 workers who engaged in the over 1,600 reported protests in 1990 amounted to only one in every 3,740 workers (*FBIS*, August 29, 1991, 31, from Agence France Presse).

8
Instability in Rural China

Thomas P. Bernstein

As early as 1987, the magazine *Liaowang* wrote of the "rebellious psychology" (*xinli zaofan*) among peasants, a characterization reiterated in a Ministry of Agriculture report in 1990.[1] Six major sources of discontent can be identified:

• *High taxes*. The "peasants' burdens" (*nongmin de fudan*) takes pride of place as the source of discontent. Apart from paying taxes to the state, peasants have financial obligations to the village and the township (*santi wutong)* designed to fund collective and governmental activities. These payments are not supposed to exceed 5 percent of net per capita incomes but have often done so. Additional "above-quota" fees, fines, and apportionments, the *sanluan* or "three chaotics" imposed by local officials and higher-level bureaucratic agencies, are an even greater source of grievance. These exactions are arbitrary, unpredictable, and open ended. They are easily manipulated by officials. Numerous peasant households have been ruined by the various exactions. The Central authorities have long recognized the threat to stability posed by excessive burdens and have made vigorous efforts to bring them under control, but they have always "rebounded" (*fantan*). The underlying problem is not simply corruption or malfeasance, but the fiscal stringency under which China's bloated administrative apparatus operates and the intense pressure to achieve rapid modernization.

The burden problem is greatest in "agricultural China" (i.e., those parts of the countryside, mainly in the central and western provinces that lack flourishing township and village industries [TVE], most of which are concentrated in the eastern belt of provinces). Some TVE profits have long been used to fund collective, welfare, and social services, particularly education. In contrast, when peasant payments to the village and township constitute the major source of revenue, officials are more likely to squeeze the peasants for money.

• *Low grain prices.* Ever since the state lowered procurement prices in 1985, which, together with inflation, made it increasingly unprofitable to farm, procurement of grain and cotton has been a second major source of discontent. Farmers not only complain about the price scissors but especially about payments in IOUs (*baitiao*) rather than cash, often the result of official diversion of state procurement funds to more profitable, sometimes speculative investments. IOUs, together with the burdens, were the major cause of a series of peasant riots that swept through rural China in 1992–1993, causing alarm and even panic among Central leaders. The regime sought vigorously to eliminate IOUs and it also periodically raised procurement prices, but problems on this front have persisted.[2]

• *Taking peasant land.* Rural industrialization requires land. Capacity to provide cheap land is a major factor in a locality's ability to attract outside investors. Often, as in numerous cases reported from Guangdong or in suburban villages of major cities in the interior, such as Zhengzhou in Honan, peasants have rioted against officials who paid little or no compensation for requisitioned land or who failed to provide dispossessed families with jobs in the new industries.[3]

• *Pollution.* Unrestrained rural industrialization has led to contamination of the water supply, poisoning of fields, and illness among TVE workers. In the absence of adequate enforcement of environmental statutes, enterprises, both collective and state, often fail to pay compensation or to eliminate the source of pollution, provoking confrontations, including riots.[4]

• *Cultural and social conflicts.* The regime seeks to suppress the spread of unapproved religious sects, fearing that as in the past, heterodox religious sects can become the basis for rebellion. (An immense nineteenth-century rebellion, the Taipings, was started, it is worth noting by someone who claimed to be the younger brother of Jesus Christ.) The regime's tolerance for revived clan and lineage activities is also limited. Government intervention has led to conflicts. The policy of requiring cremation of the dead—designed to conserve scarce arable land—which runs counter to ancient customs, also causes conflict. The most important source of conflict is over enforcement of birth control rules, particularly when cadres unfairly allocate birth quotas.[5]

• *Abusive officials.* Grievances can be caused by Central policy (e.g., in the case of procurement prices or birth control, or by local policies and practices), as in the case of burdens or IOUs. Regardless of the source, it is the process of implementation that enormously aggravates discontent.

• Relations between peasants and local officials, mainly township officials but also including village cadres have greatly deteriorated in the past decade. The sources are corruption, "use of power for private gain," and the use of brute force by local officials and police. Some of the abuses can be explained by the difficulties of enforcing unpopular policies, which rose with decollectivization and the increased possibilities for evasion that it offered, but also by the extreme pressures under which local officials labor to meet quantitative goals imposed by the higher levels.[6]

Scope and Frequency of Confrontations

When conflicts escalate, ensuing confrontations can take a variety of forms: Demonstrations; violent altercations between individual peasants and cadres; riots; wrecking of Party-government compounds; setting up of road blocks; sit-ins; holding officials captive; blocking of railroads; burning automobiles; and killing of cadres or police.

• *Variable scope.* At the low end of the spectrum, there are numerous individual incidents, often acts of revenge (e.g., the torching of a cadres' house but also suicides, of which quite a number have been reported).[7] At the high end, large-scale riots with thousands of participants involving participants from several townships have occurred. The best known is that of Renshou County, Sichuan, where riots took place in January and again in May and June 1993 with the involvement of 10–15,000 villagers from two townships.

• *Frequency.* Aggregate statistics on confrontations have been published by Hong Kong magazines based on internal sources. In contrast, Mainland sources tend to describe individual cases or to speak in general terms about rural grievances. Hong Kong sources pose problems of definition, evaluation, and accuracy, but nonetheless sound plausible in the light of complementary Mainland sources. In 1993, according to *Zheng Ming*, 6,230 cases of turmoil (*dongluan*) occurred in the countryside. In 830 of these, 500 or more people took part and more than one township was involved. In 78 cases, over a thousand participated and in

21, more than 5,000. These affected several townships and spread beyond one county. Serious disturbances included burning of county and township offices of party and government, public security, and banks. Eight thousand two hundred injuries or deaths of officials and peasants resulted, as well as 200 million RMB in damage. In 340 cases, public security, PAP (*wujing*) or local garrison units were required to pacify the populace. These forces suffered 2,400 casualties, including 385 deaths.[8]

In the first four months of 1994, incidents similar to those of 1993 erupted at roughly the same rate as in that year.[9] In the fall of 1995, confrontations occurred in eighty townships or villages in twenty-two counties in Shanxi, Henan, and Hunan, involving an aggregate of 100,000 peasants. Violent clashes reportedly took 100 odd lives, including those of 30 officials and 70 peasants. Peasants hurled rocks and Molotov cocktails.[10] In the fall, winter, and early spring of 1996–1997, confrontations in the form of demonstrations (*youxing* and *shiwei* as well as petitioning *qingyuan*) erupted in nine provinces in thirty-six counties. Two hundred and thirty were labeled cases of turmoil or rebellion (*dongluang, saoluan, baodong*.[11]

Between mid-May and mid-June 1997, another major wave of unrest arose in Hunan, Hubei, Anhui, Jiangxi, involving half a million participants. These all had similar characteristics:

• Hubei: Between May 14–19, 120,000 peasants in sixty townships in four counties in Jingzhou prefecture staged seventy-odd demonstrations in opposition to peasant exploitation and official appropriation of peasant fruits of labor. In Tianmen county, 3,000 villagers attacked County Party and government buildings; nintey injuries resulted.

• Hunan: Between May 17–22, in Yiyang and Changde prefectures, 200,000 peasants in eighty townships in five counties staged eighty incidents of assembly (*jihui*), demonstrations and submission of petitions. In several instances, peasants burned vehicles and attacked county governments elsewhere. Three deaths and fifty-four injuries resulted.

• Jiangxi: From mid-May to mid-June, 100,000 peasants in three prefectures—Jiujiang, Yichun, and Jian—in seventy townships in five counties staged a hundred protests. Peasants occupied county Party and government buildings, attacked Supply and Marketing cooperatives, plundering fertilizer and cement. In Yifeng County, 800 people attacked the Public Security bureau.

In some cases, leading cadres from the province and the prefecture were surrounded and had to be rescued by the military.

• Anhui: From May 20 to June 17, nearly 70,000 villagers living in forty townships in five counties in three prefectures staged sixty-odd incidents. Aside from attacks on official buildings, in two counties, peasants seized guns and ammunition. In Xiaoxian, 500 blocked a cargo train and seized goods, resulting in armed confrontation with the Public Security branch of the railroads. The cost was forty injuries and eleven deaths, five of whom were Public Security.[12]

Analyzing Peasant Protest

At least five questions can be asked: Who initiates the confrontation and how long do they last? What evidence is there of leadership and organization? What evidence is there that protests spread from one place to another? Are the goals of the protests to secure relief from oppressive practices, such as ruinous taxation, or are broader political goals involved?

• *Many protests are short-lived.* Many of the confrontations seem to be short-lived spontaneous eruptions in response to the latest official outrage that constitutes the straw that breaks the camel's back. Peasants embark on a rampage when accumulated anger, frustration, and resentment boil over. This happens, for instance, when a village is invaded by township officials and their retinues—public security members or simply hired thugs—to collect money from households allegedly in arrears. Such cases may include confiscation of furniture or livestock, tying up and beating of peasants, or pulling down houses leading to violence. An example of a large collective response occurred in December 1994, in Hua county, Henan. The government of a poor township government sought to raise funds for road repair, dredging of a river, and schools. The per capita exaction amounted to 120–145 yuan per capita to be handed over in three days otherwise the school would close and heads of household would be sent to a study class. The township organized small teams in order to forcibly collect the money. In response, nearly a thousand peasants attacked the township government.[13] Such protests seem to last only a few days. As Shanin writes, peasant riots consist of "short outbursts of accumulated frustration and rebellious feelings" followed by renewed quiescence.[14]

• *Some protests are organized.* In addition to spontaneous eruptions, villagers also take more planned collective initiatives to secure redress which require organization. One form of this is collective petitioning (*jiti shangfang* or *qingyuan*), in which groups of peasants go to the township or county Party and government headquarters, sometimes to the province, to present petitions demanding a hearing. Peaceful collective visits may escalate into violent collective action when officials refuse to meet with the leaders, fop them off with empty, placating promises of investigations or give them the bureaucratic runaround. Anger mounts, protests become increasingly vociferous and more villagers arrive to reenforce their vanguard. Public Security officials order the group to disperse and violence ensues. In Qidong County, Hunan, thousands of peasants petitioned authorities in five townships to reduce taxes. Clashes ensued. Public security officers used tear gas; peasants smashed township offices.[15]

• *Informal leaders*. Collective petitions require leaders, and indeed, rural China seems capable of generating leaders willing and able to lead, initiate, and even to organize collective protest. Who are the leaders? Reportedly, "in almost all the serious incidents in Shanxi, Henan, and Hunan, the 'ringleaders' were local cadres" while in some villages and townships, virtually the entire cadre force was guilty of inciting to riot.[16] In Jiangxi in 1997, township and village party and government cadres "participated in and encouraged peasants to protest (*shiwei*)."[17] Unquestionably, some grassroots cadres identify with ordinary peasants to the point of leading collective actions. At the same time, the widespread estrangement between cadres and peasants noted above suggests that cadre leadership of collective actions is not likely to be the general pattern. There are a good many accounts that indicate severe conflict between village cadres and peasants in which peasants mobilize against them.[18] Competitive village elections are supposed to bring peasants and village cadres closer together and might increase the probability that elected chairmen might organize the collective defense of peasant interests but no evidence on this point seems to exist (see also below).

• *Case: informal leaders in Renshou County*. In the January 1993 turmoil in Renshou County, Sichuan, Zhang De'an, an educated 50 year-old PLA veteran who "knew state policies and law," and who had often argued with township and village cadres over burdens, confronted officials with the existence of Central rules that would not have permitted imposition of the latest County exaction, namely a fee for the construction of a road to Chengdu. "As Zhang had the nerve to confront officials and speak the minds of the broad mass of peasants, he was universally supported." In January 1993, he was elected to the local people's congress, apparently with the largest number of votes. The county prosecutor thereupon tried to have him arrested on a charge of tax evasion. Zhang publicly tore up the arrest warrant as 700–800 peasants carrying farm tools and rods gathered. They drove the arresting officers out of the village and burned a police vehicle. Farmers then marched to the County town, jostled into the Government compound, voicing demands for justice.[19] Provincial officials intervened and conceded that Wang had been correct in opposing the County levy.

Zhang De'an, enjoying provincial support, became a recognized "peasant leader" who in the next month negotiated "with different levels of important officials" on behalf of the peasants. Wang visited provincial, city, county departments, and made speeches "rallying the masses to resist the excessive levy and to refuse to pay the road building levies." The county was reportedly pacified by early spring.

Serious rioting resumed in late May in Renshou and reached a peak in early June. According to the Sichuan Information Office, the precipitant was an article published on May 10 in *Zhongguo Xiaofeizhe Bao* (China Consumer News) charging that Renshou County officials were continuing to conceal Central directives from villagers. The paper proclaimed: "No one is allowed to defy the Central 'Urgent Circular' " sent out in March 1973 in the wake of widespread rioting. The charge that some districts and townships had violated the new rules and used force to collect funds was implicitly confirmed by the Sichuan Information Office, which reported that the Province required local cadres "conscientiously to deal with unreasonable burdens," and promised rectification of cadre work style, corruption, and violations of law and discipline.

In May, new leaders emerged, Zhang De'an having somehow dropped out of the picture. One, named Xiang Wenqing, together with seven confederates made more than 1,000 copies of the "Consumer News" article, sold them to farmers, and posted them on walls and on the roads in a district and a township. Xiang emerged as an agitator: "The central newspaper is now supporting us. If we do not take action now, when should we? We must give them hell (*zheng si*), and we must destroy the county party committee and county government. We must organize and send 10,000 people to Beijing to lodge our complaints..." Xiang reportedly led peasants to demand refund of levies going back to the beginning of household contracting and incited a riot, in which farmers, carrying pitchforks and rods, beat cadres "whenever they saw them, attacked police, holding some hostage, smashed or burned all cars in sight—passenger vehicles invariably transported officials—and blocked traffic." Serious incidents off "beating, smashing, and looting" occurred. On June 3 and 6 "more than 10,000 people besieged and attacked government offices." In Fujia District, several thousand farmers surrounded the Party-government compound, beat forty out of sixty cadres, also attacking their homes. Order was eventually restored. Xiang Wenqin and his seven confederates were arrested but ordinary peasants were treated leniently.

• *Is there capacity to sustain organized protest?* While leaders who engage in mobilizational activity do arise, there is little evidence that villages have been able to sustain organizations that engage in collective action for prolonged periods of time. To be sure, in 1992, *Zheng Ming* described an internal CCP document on fifty-odd unregistered large mass organizations. One was an "All-China Federation of Demobilized Servicemen," which claimed to have several hundred thousand members, and whose reported mission was "to do effective work" on behalf of veterans in the rural areas, a particular focus of grievance being the compulsory return to the countryside upon demobilization. The document reportedly singled out this organization as especially dangerous because there were twenty–odd million demobilized soldiers in the countryside, who had had military training, some of whom maintained personal contacts with the regular army members.[20] Yet, nothing has been heard about this or other large organizations since then. In addition, in the disorders in Shanxi, Henan, and Hunan in the fall of 1995, underground organizations reportedly fomented unrest by coordinating protest activity among several villages, but further evidence has not, but again, nothing more is known of this.[21]

• *Remedial demands.* One set of data suggests that when the regime takes steps to redress grievances (e.g., by lowering burdens), peasants are satisfied. Thus, many of the cases lack an explicitly political component, although engaging in collective action against the authorities is of course in itself a political act. Instead, peasants want to restore a proper balance between the claims of the state and their own. As a young Shandong peasant said: "It is both reasonable and lawful for farmers to pay public grain (taxes). We farmers are not confused about this. But they just take money from us in some muddled way. We give grain and don't know in which 'lord's (*laoye*) pocket it ends up in."[22] This mindset builds on a long tradition of tax resistance in which one component is peasant demands for an end to arbitrary imposts and official recognition that these demands were legitimate.[23] In the PRC, on the official side, there is an understanding that peasants had something of a right to protest against excessive taxes. Numerous Central documents and statements write understandingly of "unreasonable burdens" (*buheli de fudan*) and of "officials driving the people to revolt" (*guanbi minfan*). Lianjiang Li and Kevin O'Brien's concept of "rightful" resistance fits very well into this framework.[24]

• *Alignment of peasants with Central authorities against local officials.* The most important indicator that peasants are not opposed to the regime as such is their invocation of Central policies against local officials. This point emerges with striking clarity in the Renshou riots of 1993, discussed above. The Qidong, Hunan riots in September 1996 were also precipitated by the contrast between the limits set by higher-level, provincial document on burden relief and the levies extracted by township governments. One peasant slogan was "implement the provincial party committee's Document no. 9, relieve the peasants' burden."[25]

By publicly supporting peasants on burdens as well as on IOUs, the regime encourages peasants to assert themselves against local officials. But often there are no peaceful channels available to peasants to assert their rights. When this is the case, the Center's encouragement in effect translates into incitement to riot, or, at the very least, into undermining the authority of local officialdom. As State Council officials warned in the fall of 1993, after this pattern had played itself out, "under no circumstances should we set grass-roots level cadres against the vast number of peasants."[26]

• *Political demands.* The main indicator that some of the protests contain political demands comes in the form of slogans. In August 1993, 2,000 odd villagers from seven villages in Qingyan and Ningguo prefectures in southern Anhui held prolonged (*lianxu*) meetings to protest issuance of IOUs and government payments in kind rather than cash. Some township cadres took part, displaying banners that read: "All power to the farmers,"(*yiqie quanli gui nongmin*); "down with the new landlords of the 1990s," [oppose] "the ten thousand taxes of the Communist Party" (*gongchandang wan shui).* In one village, a "Farmers Autonomous Committee" detained members of a county Party Committee, demanded a 50 percent tax reduction, dismissal of the township head and of xiang Party Committee, as well as dissolution of township militia.[27] In the 1995 riots in Shanxi, Henan, and Hunan, slogans put forth by Party cadres read: "All wealth of the land belongs to the peasants," "end the exploitation and oppression of the peasant class," "Long live the peasant Communist Party," and "Long live the unity of the peasant class." Some villages set up "Peasant unity committees," "peasant revolutionary committees," "Autonomous peasant welfare governments," and "Peasant revolutionary command councils."[28] And in 1997, in Jiangxi, some xiang and village cadres put up these slogans: "Down with the urban exploiting class"; "divide the wealth of the new rural despots"; and "establish peasant political power."[29] All these slogans reflect demands for the right of peasants to organize independently.

Prospects for Rural Stability

Four scenarios are possible:

- First, the regime will succeed in pacifying the countryside by adopting new policies and promoting rural political reform.
- Second, rural unrest will persist in its present main form, that is, of spontaneous and organized protests in widely separated communities, constituting a significant but not unmanageable problem for the regime.
- Third, rural unrest will spread, as participants acquire increasingly sophisticated capacities to coordinate and organize protest movements.
- Fourth, rural protest movements will link up with urban counterparts, thereby posing a revolutionary challenge.

New Policies

These would aim at reducing or eliminating the structural sources of grievance. The challenge for policy makers is to design new approaches to the countryside, particularly for those parts that are primarily agricultural and or very poor: How will rural development be funded? How can an equitable system of taxation be developed that is able to pay for rural development and especially rural education in the poorer and agriculture-dependent areas of China? How can the redistributive capacities of the Center be enhanced without at least in the short run putting more pressure on local finances? (The 1993–94 tax reform, which was designed to increase the flow of revenue from the localities to the Center, worsened the financial situation of counties and townships, probably contributing to a rise in burdens.)

And, how will a more balanced approach to rural economic development be developed, one that does not simply aim at rural industrialization regardless of cost, but pays adequate attention to agricultural investment and incentives for farmers? The price scissors, IOUs, land requisitioning, and pollution are all related to the priority given to industry and to the incentives that rural officials have to "emphasize industry and neglect agriculture" (*zhonggong qingnong*). Yet, at the same time, rural industrialization with its resulting increase in local resources also offers a solution to the major grievances. Most important, how can a weak Center strengthen its capacities to secure compliance from local officials at the county and township levels? These are issues that the regime has been grappling with in the 1990s, but there are few signs that a breakthrough on any of them is in the offing. Hence, there is a substantial probability that the underlying sources of peasant grievances will persist and therefore protest as well.

Will Political Reform Increase Stability?

Effective reforms on this front would reduce or eliminate local abuses of power. Chinese leaders have in fact been engaged for some time in the reform of basic-level rural political institutions. These include building a legal structure and promoting popular consciousness of legal rights and duties (e.g., by means of the distribution of huge numbers of simple booklets on law). With regard to burdens, each household is supposed to receive "burden cards" that inform them of the amounts and limits of their obligations. Local communities are supposed to make their finances public in order to curb corruption. Such measures have encouraged the rise of a "rights consciousness" in the countryside, as Li and O'Brien have shown. As such measures take hold, they can be expected to enhance the capacity of villagers peacefully to defend their interests. Yet, the gap between goals and reality continues to be wide. For instance, a law on agriculture passed in 1993 empowers peasants to "refuse" to pay illegal levies, without, however, specifying how they can do this. The Administrative Litigation Law does not seem to be very effective with regard to tax cases.[30]

Contested village elections resulting in accountable village leaders are the most extensively publicized measure of political reform, often seen as harbingers of China's democratization. Research has largely focused on electoral procedures rather than on the crucial question of whether elected village leaders are able to alleviate the grievances highlighted in this paper. The regime hopes that leaders will be elected who have high standing in the village and who, because of their honesty and fairness, will be able to gain the cooperation of villages in the implementation of unpopular policies, such as family planning procurement, and taxation.[31] In particular, making village finance public and involving peasants in the village assembly in decisions with regard to village finances, including burden imposition, may indeed be a way of reducing conflict between cadres and peasants. An example comes from the Renshou riot. Renshou residents reportedly sought to enlist the help of peasants in neighboring Pengshan County in their protest movement. But in Pengshan village committees had put the road tax—the precipitant of the Renshou conflict—to a vote by the village representative assembly. Because the assembly had approved the tax, they refused to join in the riot. As Epstein notes, advocates of village elections in China use this example to demonstrate the impact of elections on the maintenance of stability.[32]

It seems likely that where genuine village elections have been conducted that the village-level exactions can be held within the prescribed limits. But it is important to bear in mind that the most important source of grievance lies in exactions demanded by higher administrative units. Li and O'Brien note that an elected village head may in fact have greater leverage in dealing with township and county officials, but further research is needed on this crucial point.[33]

The very continuity of rural protest right up to the present suggests that the new political institutions that are being built have not as yet had much effect. Hopefully this will change, but until it does persistence of unrest is likely.

Protests May Be Spreading

Even if the frequency of protests were to stay the same, their impact may increase if protestors in one community can link up and coordinate with their counterparts elsewhere. In some of the protests described above, disorders spread to several townships within the same county. In Gaozhou City, Guangdong, protests against family planning fines quickly spread to thirty towns.[34] In others, protests broke out in adjoining or nearby counties at about the same time. In Shanxi, for instance, all five of the counties where cluster riots erupted are located in the southwest and all were in October 1995. These incidents may be straws in the wind of a wider pattern, including contagion effects and perhaps horizontal communications and coordination (see map).

On a larger scale, the extent of simultaneity in the timing of the outbreaks is striking: Protests erupted in the winter of 1992–93, the fall of

Map 1. Approximate location of disturbances in Shanxi and Henan provinces, October 1995; and Anhui, Hubei, Hunan, and Jiangxi in May–June 1997, showing proximity in three provinces.

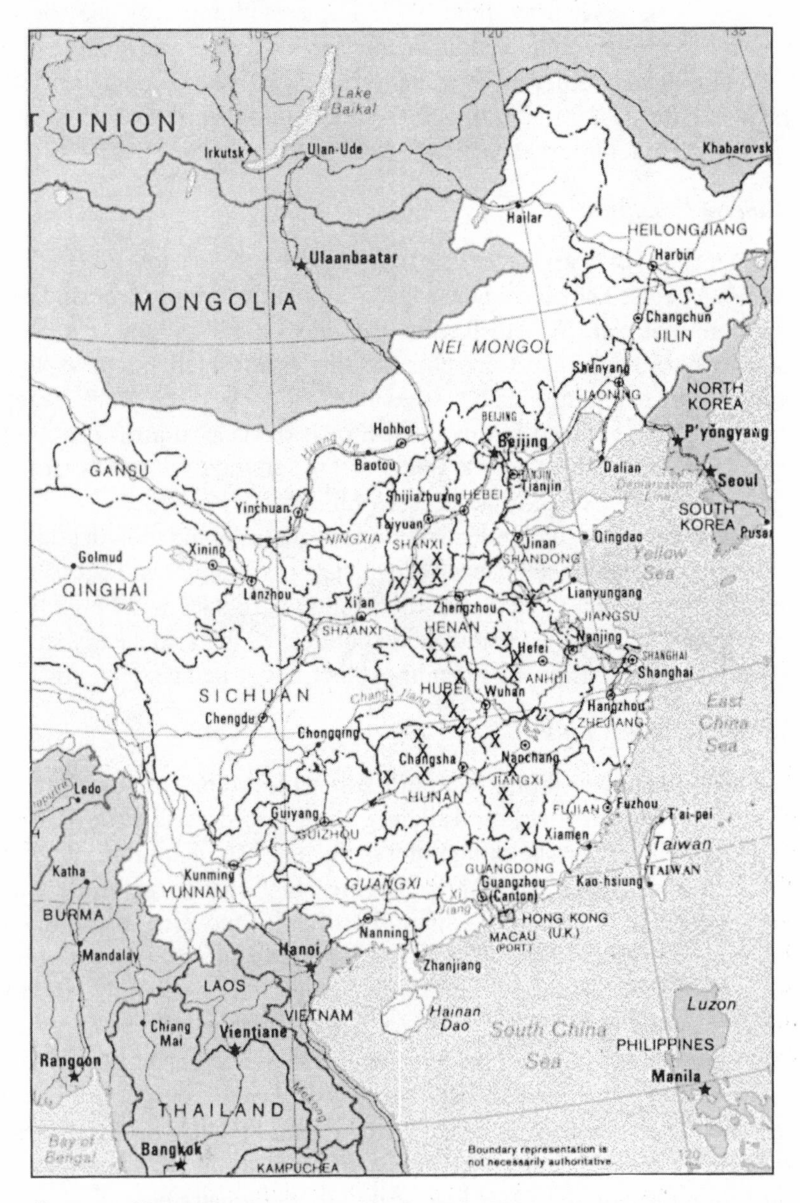

Sources: China Perspectives, no. 3, Jan.–Feb. 1996, p. 7, and *Zheng Ming*, no. 8, August 1997, pp. 19–21.

1995, the fall 1996, and in May–June 1997. Villages experiencing similar oppressive conditions may well react in similar ways, but why in a span of a few weeks, as in May–June 1997? The agricultural cycle may be the reason but another could be that we are seeing greater coordination. As long as protests do not erupt at the same time, the regime can handle them seriatim, but if the rioting does break out on an increasing territorial scale, the regime's capacity to restore order may be stretched.

Modern Communication

Villagers have increased access to newspapers, to television, and to Central documents. They have new capacities locally to reproduce and disseminate material. In both Renshou, Sichuan, and Qidong, Hunan, a thousand or so copies of Central or provincial documents or newspaper articles were made and sold or posted in the villages. In one of the Jiangxi cases, a peasant ruined by his township secretary's ruthless exactions "specially phoned the Central Television programme 'Focus of Coverage' " in the hope of getting his case publicized.[35]

Access to means of communication contributes to the mobilization of villagers, enhancing their capacity to contact one another and coordinate activities. As China modernizes, the country's villages will be increasingly integrated into the national body politic, and this will clearly stimulate rural political activism, including, other things being equal, protest.

No Urban-Rural Link

The least likely possibility is an urban-rural link-up. The literature on revolution views an urban-rural alliance as a key to success. In the present case, the major, overwhelming point is the absence of appropriate linkages between urban and rural protest. Those in the urban sector, students and intellectuals, who are the natural leaders of movements aiming at political change, have not demonstrated serious interest in rural grievances or in making contact with rural people. The classic illustration is the Tiananmen movement in 1989, when, as Elizabeth Perry observes, urban protestors failed to take advantage of peasant capacities for collective action.[36] Intellectuals have strongly elitist attitudes. They disdain peasants. They blame Mao's despotism on their "feudal" backwardness. Some fear China's uncontrolled peasant masses, as the 1994 book, *Viewing China through the Third Eye*, strikingly demonstrates.

The underlying obstacle to urban-rural cooperation are the deep cleavages between the two sectors that developed during the Mao era and that continue to persist in terms of privileges, wealth, and social status. On the rural side of the divide, there is much evidence of resentment of the urban sector, as the slogan "down with the urban bureaucratic exploiting class" mentioned above suggests. Most of the other slogans called for peasant autonomy, by implication from the urban sector.

Current developments—reform of the state industrial sector—will probably further fan urban-rural tensions. As more and more state-sector workers become unemployed, competition for jobs with the migrant population is likely to increase. It is already leading to new restrictions on migration and forced return to the countryside. Resentment of the urban sector will no doubt increase. In sum, the future is likely to see continued rural unrest with a possibility of escalation to a more coherent and organized level.

Notes

1. *Liaowang*, no. 8, February 23, 1987, and Zonghe Jihua Si, "Guanyu nongmin fudan de diaocha," (Investigation of peasant burdens), *Nongye Jingji Wenti*, no. 2, 1990, p. 60.

2. On IOUs, see Andrew Wedeman, "Stealing from Farmers: Institutional Corruption and the 1992 IOU Crisis," *China Quarterly* (CQ) no. 152, December 1997, pp. 805–831. For a recent article on the price scissors, see *Renmin Ribao* (*RMRB*),overseas-ed, June 1, 1998.

3. See Wu Jieh-min, unpublished dissertation, Columbia University, May 1998, and *Shih-chieh Jih-pao* (*SCJP*), September 18, 1997 and March 27, 1998.

4. The first of many such cases occurred in the Beijing suburbs in 1988; see Agence France Press, Hong Kong, July 1, 1988 and Xinhua, Beijing, June 30, 1988, both in *FBIS* no.127, pp.17–18.

5. On clan conflicts involving government, see Kyodo, Tokyo, October 27, 1992, *FBIS* no. 92, p. 57. On a riot precipitated by government suppression of a large parade from a local goddess, see Fuzhou Radio, August 22, 1988, in *FBIS* no. 88, p. 46. On resistance to birth planning, see *Ming Pao*, Hong Kong, September 7, 1997, in BBC-FE/3021, p. G/4, September 11, 1997.

6. For some major articles, see *Nongmin Ribao* (*NMRB*), September 26, 1988 and August 22, 1992, Wang Zhongru, "*Weixian de lie hen: Nongcun dangqun guanxi shuli*," (The danger of a rift: estranged relations between party and masses), *Shehui*, no. 2, 1990, pp. 9–11, and *Zhongguo Qingnian Bao*, January 27, 1994, *FBIS* no. 94, pp. 2–3.

7. On two recent cases, see *Fazhi Bao*, April 10,1996 and June 7, 1996.

8. Lu Nong, "Nongcun bu wending qingkuang ehua," *Zheng Ming*, Hong Kong, no. 8, August 1994, pp. 28–29. Lu writes of a total of 1.67 million cases but the meaning is not clear.

9. Ibid.

10. "Peasant Riots in Shanxi, Henan, and Hunan," *China Perspective*, no. 2, January–February, 1996, pp. 6–9, reproduced from *Dongxiang* no. 124, December 1995, pp. 18–19.

11. Li Zijing, "*Si sheng wushi wan nongmin kangzheng*," (Half a million peasants resist in four provinces), *Zheng Ming*, no. 8, 1997, pp. 19–21, reproduced from *Dongxiang*, April 1997. Confrontations in nine provinces took place in the winter and spring of 1996–1997; the four refers to the main story on riots in May–June 1997. See *SCJP*, November 11, 1996, for disturbances in Qidong county, Hunan, in September 1996.

12. Li Zijing, ibid.

13. Wang Yanbin, "*Nongmin fudan: Anxia hulu qilai piao*," (Peasant burdens: Solving one problem only to have another one crop up). *Minzhu yu Fazhi*, no.13, July 6, 1995, pp.11–13.

14. Theodore Shanin,"The Peasantry as a Political Factor," in T. Shanin, ed., *Peasants and Peasant Societies* (Baltimore, MD: Penguin Books, 1971): p. 258.

15. *Ming Pao*, November 8, 1996, BBC-FE, no. 2765, pp. G/4–5 and *SCJP*, November 11, 1996.

16. See footnote 10, supra.

17. Li Zijing *op.cit.*

18. Chen Daolong, "Xiangcun zai huhan: nongmin fudan wenti shilu," (The village cries out: A record of the burden problem), *Yu Hua*, Supplement, 1994, pp. 2–22.

19. This account is taken from the author's, "In Quest of Voice: China's Farmers and Prospects for Political Liberalization," paper presented to the Columbia University Seminar on Modern China, February 10, 1994, pp. 70–77. The major sources are: *Hsin Pao*, Hong Kong, April 20, 1993, *FBIS* 81, pp. 10–12; *Zhongguo Xinwen She*. Beijing, June 12, 1993, *FBIS* 112, pp. 28–29; and Jung Sheng, "Great Impact of Ag Issue—Tracking Incident of Peasant Riots in Sichuan's Renshou County," *Hsin Pao*, Hong Kong, June 10, 1993, *FBIS* 111, pp. 10–15.

20. Yang Po, "*Zhonggong yanfang minjian zuzhi*," (The CCP strictly guards against popular organizations), *Cheng Ming*, Hong Kong, no. 6, 1992, pp. 26–27.

21. See footnote 10, supra.

22. *NMRB*, January 20, 1988

23. See R. Bin Wong, *China Transformed: Historical Change and the Limits of European Experience*, (Ithaca: Cornell Press, 1997, chpt.10 on tax resistance).

24. Lianjiang Li and Kevin J.O'Brien, "Villagers and Popular Resistance in Contemporary China," *Modern China*, vol. 22, no. 1, January 1996, pp. 28–61. See also O'Brien and Li, "The Politics of Lodging Complaints in China, CQ no.143, September 1995, pp. 756–783.

25. *Ming Pao*, November 8, 1996, *op.cit.*

26. Yuan Mu and Yang Yongzhe in *RMRB* September 17, 1993. *FBIS* no.199, p. 38.

27. "*Anhui nongmin kangshui shijian*," *Cheng Ming*, no. 9, September 1993, p. 93.

28. See note 10, supra.

29. Li Zijing, *op.cit.*

30. See Xin-min Pei, "Citizens vs. Mandarins: Administrative Litigation in

China," *CQ* no.152, December 1997, pp. 832–862. There are some cases of peasants successfully suing in county courts for burden relief.

31. See Daniel Kelliher, "The Chinese Debate over Village Self Government," *China Journal*, no. 37, pp. 1–24.

32. Amy B. Epstein, "Village Elections in China: Experimenting with Democracy," in US Congress, Joint Economic Committee, *China's Economic Future: Challenges to US Policy* (Washington, GPO,1996, p. 416).

33. Lianjiang Li and Kevin J. O'Brien, "The Struggle over Village Elections," in Roderick MacFarquhar and Merle Goldman, eds. *The Paradox of Post-Mao Reforms* (Cambridge, MA, Harvard University Press, forthcoming).

34. *Ming Pao*, September 7, 1997, BBC-FE/3021, pp. G/4–5.

35. *Ping Kuo Jih Pao*, November 25, 1996, BBC-FE/2783, pp. G/4–5. The Chinese name of the program is "*Jiaodian fangtan jiemu*," see *SCJP*, November 26, 1996.

36. Elizabeth Perry, "Casting a Chinese 'Democracy' Movement: The Role of Students, Workers, and Entrepreneurs," in Jeffrey Wasserstrom and Elizabeth Perry, eds. *Popular Protest and Political Culture in China* (Boulder: Westview Press, 2nd ed.), pp. 74–92.

9

The Potential for Instability Among Alienated Intellectuals and Students in Post-Mao China

Merle Goldman

Although the Communist party-state, led by Mao Zedong, had persecuted China's intellectuals from the mid-1950s until Mao's death in 1976, the intellectuals welcomed the post-Mao party-state, inaugurated in 1978 and led by Mao's Long March colleague Deng Xiaoping. Despite their repression under Mao, like their literati predecessors, they saw themselves as members of the governing elite and as advisors to the political leadership. For the most part, the post-Mao governments of Deng Xiaoping (1978–92) and Jiang Zemin shared their Confucian view of the importance of intellectuals to good governance. Deng and his supposed successor, the reformist general-secretary Hu Yaobang rehabilitated virtually all the intellectuals purged by Mao from the prisons, labor reform camps and "stinking 9th hell" in which Mao had put them. They appointed them to positions in government as well as in academia and the media and accorded them the prestige and high offices once accorded the literati. Most intellectuals reciprocated by helping the post-Mao party-state repudiate the ideology and policies of the Mao era and move toward a more open society and market economy. They enthusiastically joined the official establishment and supported the Deng Xiaoping and the succeeding Jiang Zemin governments.

Nevertheless, an influential, but small number of intellectuals on either side of the political spectrum, liberal and Maoist, became increasingly alienated as China's economic reforms took off. Those intellectuals, associated with the reformist leaders, by the late 1980s found themselves in conflict with the political establishment they had joined. The intellectuals, associated with Hu Yaobang, were put in charge of revising ideology, so important to any Chinese regime as a means for unifying its huge population. Since they were primarily former ideologists, editors and writers, they turned first to early Marxism and then to Western democratic ideas to fill the void left by the bankruptcy of Marxism-Leninism and Mao Thought during the Cultural Revolution. Their efforts led to a "humanist" version of Marxism without much Leninism, similar to that developing in Eastern Europe, and then in 1986, to demands for political reform culminating in student demonstrations demanding political rights. When the student demonstrations moved up the coast from the University of Science and Technology in Hefei, Anhui to Tiananmen Square, the symbolic center of China's government, the veteran Long Marchers, still a powerful political force in the Deng era, put pressure on Deng to purge Hu Yaobang in January 1987 for refusing to take action against the students and dismiss the intellectuals associated with Hu Yaobang.

In the late 1980s, a new school of thought emerged, called "neo-authoritarianism," formulated by a younger group of more technocratic intellectuals, associated with Deng's next supposed successor, Zhao Ziyang. As advisers on economic policies, they were attracted to the authoritarian political model of their ethnic and post-Confucian East Asian neighbors, the "four little dragons." Following their example, they called for several decades of economic reform under a strong centralized leader until a large educated middle-class emerged that could lead the country toward democratization. They and members of Hu Yaobang's intellectual network supported the student demonstrators in Tiananmen Square in their demands for political reform in spring 1989. When Deng purged Zhao Ziyang for refusing to go along with the imposition of martial law on May 20 and ordered the troops to crack down on the demonstrators on June 4, these highly-placed intellectuals and their followers were either imprisoned, sent to labor reform, exiled abroad, purged from the establishment, or silenced. Several of them along with scores of student leaders of the 1989 demonstrations were imprisoned for long periods of time. Thus, those on the liberal side of the political spectrum were eliminated as a source of supposed instability.

Despite the repression of scores of their colleagues, most intellectuals and students, though disillusioned with the regime because of the violent crackdown, were not alienated from it. While initially there was a return to the indoctrination and politicization of academia of the Mao era, it was short-lived. Moreover, unlike under Mao, the intellectuals, their families and friends did not suffer for the supposed "crimes" of a small number of their colleagues. They continued to work in the government bureaucracies, academia, and the media. Even their access to the outside world was not interrupted. Although Deng, under pressure from his Long March colleagues, launched a series of campaigns against Western ideas and values in the 1980s and Jiang Zemin carried out campaigns against "all-out Westernization" and peaceful evolution in the early 1990s, the campaigns did not stop the inflow of Western ideas and products. The political leadership was reluctant to back up these campaigns with the threat of violence, mass mobilization, and ideological zeal of the Mao years that had been so destabilizing. Moreover, China's growing economic and technological international interdependence made it virtually impossible to keep out influences from abroad. Most important, the creation of a market economy and opening to the outside world gave intellectuals and students, for the first time in the People's Republic, alternatives to government employment, either in the professions, non-state enterprises, foreign-joint ventures, or their own businesses, providing a degree of economic independence which gave them some protection from political retaliation.

Equally important, unlike the Mao era, intellectuals could cut themselves off from political participation if they wished. As the ideological homogeneity of the Mao era gave way to cultural and intellectual pluralism, China's large cities attracted newly-activated artists, intellectuals, writers, entertainers, audiences, foreign visitors, and students. A small number of these urban intellectuals engaged in public political discourse until the June 4, 1989 crackdown. Nevertheless private and cultural discourse among an array of diverse groups continued in the 1990s and ranged widely over a variety of subjects. Even though public political debate was suppressed through most of the 1990s, the retreat of the state from the cultural realm in terms of censorship, financial support, and tolerance of foreign influences sparked an explosion of artistic experimentation, popular culture and non-political activity in a variety of mediums. As long as the content and style of one's intellectual, cultural, and professional work stayed away from politics, the party-state tolerated and at times even encouraged apolitical culture as a diversion from political engagement.

Even the ideological and political discourse in most of the 1980s had been conducted relatively freely, except during the brief campaigns in 1981,1983, and 1987. In reaction to the Mao era, politically-engaged intellectuals outspokenly repudiated Mao's radicalism and utopianism and discussed Western Marxism and democratic liberalism. Although a number of the more conservative elders relentlessly attacked these ideas, they were unable to drown out the prevailing liberal tone of the 1980s. Some of them even participated in spirited debates with the more democratic-leaning intellectuals who likewise engaged in spirited debates with the neo-authoritarians. For the first time in the PRC, various sides of a political debate were given relatively equal treatment in prominent intellectual forums, newspapers, and journals. Until June 4 even intellectuals associated with Hu Yaobang, after brief periods of silence induced by the campaigns against them, were able to return to public life and participate in these debates, though not in the mainstream party media. But from the mid-1980s until June 4, there were a number of different vehicles through which one could express alternative views—the semi-official papers, such as the *World Economic Herald,* and non-official journals, such as *Economic Weekly.* Moreover the Hong Kong press provided another outlet for differing views, which then made their way back into China. The political discussions and debates of the 1980s influenced and inspired the student leaders of the pro-democracy 1989 demonstrations.[1]

The Jiang Zemin Era

The June 4 crackdown, the collapse of the Soviet Union, and the disorder accompanying Russia's move to democracy marked an intellectual shift away from the humanist and liberal tone of the 1980s. With the revival of Maoism in the early 1990s, instead of the Maoists being marginalized as they had been during the governments of Hu Yaobang and Zhao Ziyang, those advocating Western liberal ideas and neo-authoritarianism were marginlized. A number of Maoist ideologues or neo-leftists, led by conservative elder, Deng Liqun, returned to power in the academic and cultural spheres. They attempted to revitalize Mao worship, to foment class struggle, and to reindoctrinate the population in Marxism-Leninism. "Mao fever" (*Mao re*) spread in the early 1990s to China's major cities with the reappearance of Mao's little red books, Mao souvenirs, and Mao medallions ubiquitously hanging from taxicab rearview mirrors. The fever was also fired up by nostalgia for the supposed order and honest officials of the Mao years in contrast to the disorder and corruption of the post-Mao era.[2] At the same time, counter to China's growing entwinement with the outside world and increasing internal regionalism and diversity, the post-Deng leaders and their intellectual spokesmen reemphasized ideological and political unity.

However, when Deng took his trip south in 1992 to revive the economic reforms, he attacked the "left" as a greater danger than the right. Soon after, the Mao fever gradually subsided and in 1993–94, a more open political atmosphere emboldened some of the politically engaged intellectuals of the1980s once again to call publicly in a series of petitions for political reform and the release of political prisoners. This political spring, however, was fleeting. By the mid-1990s, all public political dissent was suppressed. At the same time, despite Deng Xiaoping's attack on the left, Deng Liqun and his spokesmen, in four "ten-thousand word" public statements, persisted in taking a Maoist approach, specifically in their call for the continuation of the state-controlled economy, which had strong support in the bureaucracy, particularly in the planning ministries. Their statements warned that the decline of state industries would help capitalism prevail over socialism and would impoverish the workers. In opposition to Deng's non-ideological approach, they continued to stress the ongoing struggle between capitalism and socialism. Though criticized and pushed to the margins once again, as the post-Deng leadership moved in the late 1990s to reform state industries, the neo-leftists continued to speak out publicly through several journals that explicitly expressed their viewpoint.

Another intellectual strain of the mid-1990s was neo-conservatism. While promoted by government spokesmen, it was also spontaneously propounded by intellectuals, particularly a growing number of younger intellectuals in reaction to the pro-Western, anti-traditional discourse of the 1980s, when disillusionment with Maoism had instilled an unreasoned idealism about Western societies and political life. But as intellectuals and returned students learned more about the West and came in closer contact with its realities, their idealism waned. Consequently, in the 1990s, a younger generation of intellectuals, who came of age in the post-Mao era, some of whom were close to the children of the party elders, the "princelings," moved to another extreme. Like the neo-authoritarians of the late 1980s, they did not refer to Marxism-Leninism, but unlike them, they did not endorse a full scale move to the market and development of a middle class that eventually would lead China toward democracy. Rather, like the neo-leftists, they decried the decentralization that had accompanied China's move to the market and called for tighter central controls over the economic regions and cultural life. In addition, they urged that the millions of migrants, coming into the cities in search of economic opportunities, be returned to their villages.

However, whereas the neo-leftists had argued for a reassertion of a state-owned, recentralized economy in ideological terms, the neo-conservatives argued for it in practical terms—a strong central state was necessary to ensure stability. Without a restrengthening of party-state controls, they asserted, the party would be unable to handle the social instabilities caused by the economic reforms and internal migrants. Unless the erosion of the party-state were stopped, they warned that chaos, *luan*, the traditional Chinese nightmare, would result. The popular book *Looking at China through a Third Eye* (Disanzhi yanjing kan Zhongguo), published in 1994, and the journal, *Strategy and Management* (Zhanlue yu guanli) were representative of the neo-conservative view. They implicitly criticized Deng's reforms for weakening the central government.

Accompanying the reaction against Western liberalism was a revival of neo-Confucianism. Although its proponents did not refer to Marxism-Leninism, the leadership found their views more in tune with their own goals than the views of the neo-leftists or democrats. The neo-Confucianists asserted that modernization did not mean Westernization. In fact, the seeds of modernization, they argued, could be found in Chinese history and values, specifically in Confucianism. Instead of China's deeply-embedded traditional culture being an obstacle to its modernization, as preached by the May Fourth intellectuals and party reformers and intellectuals in the 1980s, they insisted that Confucianism was conducive to modernization. Citing the dynamic economies of the Confucian-shaped societies of their East Asian neighbors, they asserted that a revived neo-Confucianism could provide the intellectual and cultural underpinnings for China's rapid economic development while helping China avoid the immorality and individualism of Western capitalism.

To buttress the demand for increasing political centralization, the Jiang leadership encouraged a spirit of nationalism as leaders earlier in the century did to promote national unity. A rising tide of nationalist sentiment in the mid-1990s cut across all schools of thought—neo-leftist, neo-conservative, and neo-Confucian—with the exception of the virtually silenced school of democratic thought. Despite Deng Liqun and his allies' efforts,

Jiang Zemin merely paid lip service to reviving Marxism-Leninism and Mao Thought. He stressed building "socialist spiritual civilization," but this concept had little to do with socialism. Though concerned with polite behavior in public places, its major emphasis was on China's revival as a great civilization. The leadership agreed with the neo-Confucians that Confucianism was relevant to the present and like them, stressed its authoritarian values and hierarchical society rather than other Confucian teachings, such as the intellectuals' obligation to criticize officials who abused power or engage in unfair treatment of the population.

Generally, the leadership's nationalist emphasis was readily embraced by the younger generation of intellectuals and urban youth. They needed little prodding. In 1993, they had spontaneously protested against the rejection of China's bid to host the International Olympics in the year 2000 which they blamed on the United States. Also China's apparent economic success had awakened nationalist pride among the youth as well as among the intellectuals. They echoed their leaders' charge that the United States was attempting to contain China's rising power. Their indignation was expressed in books like *China Can Say No* (Zhongguo keyi shuo bu) and variations on that theme, which became bestsellers in the mid-1990s.

Nevertheless, like the other happenings in post-Mao China, nationalist discourse was diverse and contradictory. Its stridency was challenged in articles in the still relatively liberal journals *Dushu* (Reading) and *Dongfeng* (The Orient) until it was forced to cease publication at the end of 1996. Moreover, in the late 1990s the leadership tried to rein in the nationalist fervor so that it not turn into xenophobia that could spin out of control with demonstrations which might undermine the party-state or antagonize other countries with which China sought trade and investment. Thus, the regime virtually banned such writings as *China Can Say No,* which were directed specifically against the United States and Japan. In addition, it stopped protestors from demanding reparations from Japan, fearing that they would ignite large-scale demonstrations that could threaten the regime as well as frighten off Japanese investors. With the improvement of relations with the United States, inaugurated by the visits of President Jiang to the United States in 1997 and President Clinton to China in 1998, the nationalist sentiment that had permeated the intellectual and student circles in the mid 1990s gradually lessened.

By century's end, as the post-Deng leadership tolerated a number of different intellectual currents, a new political springtime slowly reappeared.[3] In 1996, Liu Ji, vice president of CASS and an advisor to Jiang, sponsored publication of *Heart to Heart Talks with the General Secretary,* which gave Jiang a reformist image and criticized the nationalist, leftist discourse of the mid-1990s. Even before the 15th Party Congress in October 1997 when Jiang called for reform of state industry, an economist at Beijing University, Shang Dewan, sent several letters to the Central Committee in the summer of 1997 calling for political reform. Although Jiang at the Congress also called for political reform, he did not spell out what he meant by political reform. Nevertheless, following the lead of the political leadership, after the Congress several highly-placed academics provided the rationale and more details. An advisor on state industry reform, the economist, Deng Furong publicly pointed out that economic reforms could not be sustained without political reforms; the only way to deal with the rising unemployment, widening income gaps, pollution, and corruption, he insisted, was to develop democracy. A provincial reform official turned business man, Fang Jue, distributed a statement calling for democratic reforms based on the Western system of checks and balances. The former head of the American Studies Institute at CASS, Li Shenzhi contributed an article to the 10th anniversary of the journal *Reform*, explaining that contrary to the leadership's past emphasis on economic rights, that to act as a citizen one must have political and civil rights, as well as economic rights. Since China, he observed, had already made headway in providing basic economic livelihood, it should now provide political and civil rights. Counter to the neo-conservatives who insisted that civil and political rights were alien to Asia, he pointed out that the idea of such rights had been introduced into China in the early decades of the twentieth century. Therefore, the concept of universal human rights, he asserted, had already become a part of China's history.[4] Another respected economist, Mao Yushi, reaffirmed this argument in an essay entitled "Liberalism, Equal Status, and Human Rights." The fact that Jiang allowed President Clinton to talk about the indivisibility of economic rights and political rights several times over national television on his visit to China in June 1998 would indicate that the party-state may once again tolerate and even approve discussion of political reforms. At the same time, a controversial best seller *Cross Swords* (Jiaofeng), by two journalists from *People's Daily,* attacked the leftists not only for opposing reform of state industry, but also opposing China's interaction with the Western capitalist world. Though published in a series organized by Jiang adviser Liu Ji, the book provoked a counterattack by the neo-leftist journal *Contemporary Thoughts* (Dangdai Sichao), which sued the authors for quoting from the third "ten thousand word" essay without authorization and distorting the contents of the article. At the same time, large scale conferences were convened on the twentieth anniversary of the famous article "Practice is the Sole Criterion of Truth," which had launched the attack on Maoist ideas in May 1978. The leadership's speeches at the conferences appeared to be directed against the neo-Maoists in 1998. On the one hand, such a contradictory, pluralistic intellectual atmosphere made it difficult to be an alienated intellectual in the late 1990s; on the other hand, as in the late 1980s, it could also provoke students once more to demand more rights as they had in a similarly contentious atmosphere in the late 1980s.

Potential for Instability Among Alienated Intellectuals

The Jiang government's more tolerant approach to political discourse in the late 1990s indicates that it believes it can handle any student protest. While the party-state's control has weakened further in the post-Deng era due to accelerating market reforms and opening to the outside world as well as to the leadership's own withdrawal from most areas of daily life, except birth control and politics, it still remains strong enough to suppress any threat that might come from student demonstrations. It has stationed police around Beijing University and other universities to prevent demonstrations or to keep them confined within the universities. Moreover, it can act more quickly against demonstrations than in 1989 because it no longer need turn to the military for help. Since June 4, it has strengthened and modernized the People's Armed Police specifically to deal with student demonstrations much more effectively than the PAP's failed attempts in 1989. Without having to negotiate with the military, it is much easier for the party to take swift action against student demonstrations today than in the 1980s. Even without using the People's Armed Police, the party-state has been successful so far in suppressing any intellectual and student challenges on June 4th anniversaries or on any other controversial occasions, either by putting intellectuals and students under surveillance, house arrest, or detention and preventing students from gathering outside their universities. The party-state's precautions and increased ability to suppress such a protest the moment it starts lessens the threat.

Nevertheless, the Jiang government has been particularly concerned and taken preemptive action against three groups of intellectuals. One group is made up of the families of those students still imprisoned because of the 1989 demonstrations and those compiling lists of people killed in June 4. Within this group are also former officials, such as Zhao Ziyang and Bao Tong, who along with the families, have asked for a reevaluation of the 1989 demonstration. On each June 4 anniversary or on the occasion of a visit of a high foreign leader, they are literally put under a form of house detention for fear that they could use the occasion to stir up a protest which might gain popular support and get out of control. Nevertheless, such a threat seems to be diminishing. The fact that Clinton was allowed to call the June 4 crackdown "wrong" and "tragic" on Chinese television may indicate that a reevaluation is being discussed within the leadership and may slowly emerge, thereby undercutting the demand repercussions caused by a reevaluation.

The Jiang government has also quickly repressed several efforts of another group of intellectuals to organize an open opposition party by preventing them from registering the party and detaining or arresting the leaders of such a movement. The most recent occasion was in the wake of Clinton's trip, when ten of the people who had attempted to register an open opposition party during his visit were detained and their leaders arrested afterwards.

Nevertheless, the party-state might find it much more difficult to suppress intellectuals who form a coalition with the increasingly disaffected workers, who have been laid off or not paid because of the reform of state industry. The party-state has taken a much more cautious approach toward the demonstrations of workers and pensioners going on all over the country, particularly in China's rust belt—Sichuan, Shaanxi, the Northeast and Hubei in the late 1990s. Its greater caution toward workers and pensioners reflects the fear that a violent crackdown on their protests could ignite social unrest into a conflagration that would spread quickly and be difficult to contain. Particularly worrisome are the intellectuals who help workers establish independent labor movements. Ever since the Polish Solidarity labor movement developed into a political movement in 1980 with the help of intellectuals that was able to overthrow the Communist Party in Poland, China's leaders have feared a similar development in China. They have reason to fear. China's twentieth-century history is marked with instances of intellectuals and workers joining together in political movements that have caused profound changes as seen in the May Fourth Movement and most important, the establishment of the Chinese Communist Party in the 1920s.

While most intellectuals have nothing to do with workers, the politically-engaged members of the Red Guard generation, who have not been coopted by the regime, are less reluctant to join with workers in common cause. Because their education had been interrupted in the Cultural Revolution, many of the ex-Red Guard participants in the Democracy Wall movement in 1978–79 were workers who might have been intellectuals in different times. Having been forced to work in factories and fields during the Cultural Revolution, they had contacts with ordinary working people, which their intellectual predecessors and the younger generation do not have. Moreover, having become totally disillusioned with their political leaders and the political system during the Cultural Revolution, they tend to question everything. Because of that experience, some of them have had difficulty finding a niche for themselves in post-Mao China and even those who do, behave differently than their non-Red Guard colleagues.

One of the first examples of a worker-intellectual alliance in the post-Mao era was during the 1989 Tiananmen Square demonstration when a group of workers established the Beijing Workers Autonomous Federation (BWAF) that grew to 20,000 members. Apart from a small short-lived spontaneous workers movement in Taiyuan, Shanxi which carried out a strike in winter of 1980, this federation was the first independent labor organization in the PRC. Though headed by Han Dongfang, a 27–year-old railway worker, with a high school education, several intellectuals advised the union. While most students and intellectuals kept their distance from the workers during the 1989 Tiananmen demonstration, these intellectuals, who worked at the first non-state political think tank, the Social and Economic Research Institute (SERI), made contact with the union. SERI was headed by ex-Red Guards, who had participated in virtually every major demonstration beginning with the April 5, 1976, protest against the Cultural Revolution. One of its members, Li Jinjin, also a lecturer in law at Beijing University, became a legal advisor to BWAF. He wrote its constitution and defended three of its workers who were arrested during the 1989 demonstration and got them released from police custody. When martial law was imposed on May 20, the leaders of SERI sought to establish a united front with the various autonomous unions set up during the demonstration, planning to negotiate with the political leadership for a peaceful resolution of the crisis. They included the BWAF along with other autonomous groups and also sought to get the support of the official All-China Federation of Trade Unions. Their efforts to unite with workers' unions, official as well as unofficial, to challenge the party's policy came closest to fulfilling the elders' fear of an intellectual-worker alliance that would threaten the party and their political power. This emerging coalition of intellectuals and workers was perhaps the precipitating cause for Deng's decision to send in the military against the Tiananmen demonstrators on June 4.[5]

As state industries became increasingly bankrupt and as the reform of state industry got underway in 1998 with lay-offs and non-payment of wages and pensions for state workers, the party's fear of an alliance between disaffected workers and intellectuals has become palpable. As protests increased and spread, Jiang instructed local authorities to guard against intellectuals colluding with unemployed workers. News of the arrest of various intellectuals for helping workers set up independent unions in different locales has leaked out to the Hong Kong and the Western press almost weekly. So far, however, there is lack of concrete evidence and detail on these underground unions. Nevertheless, intellectuals who had been ex-Red Guards and had participated in Democracy Wall and in the 1986 and 1989 demonstrations are reported to have been sent to labor reform camps and prison for helping to set them up. It is difficult to estimate the number and size of such alliances and unions. All that is known is that they are spreading all over the country, from Xian to Wuhan and from Heilongjiang to Shenzhen.

Thus the party-state has two major fears at the end of the century. One is that discussions of political reforms in the late 1990s among establishment intellectuals might provoke student demonstrations, as they did in 1989, to demand much more than the regime is willing to allow and undermine its authority. An even more immediate concern, however, is that underground intellectual-worker alliances might emerge over-ground and become a political movement that could overthrow the regime as Solidarity did in Poland. The potential for this kind of a happening is real. If China's leaders have learned any lesson from June 4, however, it should be that gradual movement toward building political institutions, such as a genuine legislature, independent unions, rule of law, and a free press, will give disaffected elements such as laid-off workers, their former Red Guard associates and politically-concerned intellectuals and students a way to express their views so that they will not have to resort to destabilizing demonstrations and mass protests in order to air their grievances and get redress. The early signs of a political spring in the late 1990s and the fact that well-placed intellectuals have expressed such views in the public media may indicate that the leaders may be learning that lesson.

Notes

1. Geremie Barme, *Shades of Mao: The Posthumous Cult of the Great Leader*, (Armonk, N.Y., M.E. Sharpe, 1996).

2. Craig Calhoun, *Neither Gods nor Emperors: Students and the Struggle for Democracy in China*, (University of California Press, 1994).

3. Joseph Fewsmith, "Jiang Zemin Takes Command," *Current History*, September 1998.

4. *Gaige*, January 1998, pp. 13–14.

5. Merle Goldman, *Sowing the Seeds of Democracy in China* (Harvard University Press, 1994) pp. 338–360.

10
The Potential for Instability in Minority Regions

June Teufel Dreyer

Under Mao Zedong, policy toward ethnic minorities alternated between tolerant acceptance of "national minorities special characteristics" and strong pressure for complete assimilation. The former was most prominent from 1949 to 1957; from 1960 through 1965; and from 1971 until Mao's death in 1976. The latter was principally in evidence during the intervening years of the Great Leap Forward and the Cultural Revolution.

The nature of the relationship between class structure and the nationality question was hotly debated among party intellectuals. Those who favored gradualist policies took as their premise Karl Marx's view that class problems were related to nationality problems: what appeared to be ethnic antagonisms and differences would simply wither away as socialist structures removed the reasons for their existence. Marx had envisioned a gradual growing together of ethnic groups and cultures.

Less patient personalities, while never publicly arguing that Marx was wrong, felt that strong pressure was needed to effect the synthesis. The implementation of this view reached its extreme in the Cultural Revolution when Mao announced that nationality problems were not simply related to class problems: they *were* class problems. The policy directive implicit in this was clear: abolish nationality differences, and class differences would disappear as well. Socialism could be achieved quickly.

Whether accommodationist or assimilationist, these policies had certain commonalities. The end goal, that of creating a homogeneous communist/proletarian state, was the same: the principal difference was whether this state should be brought about gradually or quickly. Although the party line during periods of accommodation stressed that the homogeneous culture would be a blend of all nationalities characteristics, there was never any doubt about whose culture would predominate. Comprising 94 percent of the population and with a literacy rate far surpassing that of most minorities[1] and, it was generally felt, a vastly superior culture,[2] the Han would provide the bedrock from which the new society would emerge.

Even in periods of accommodation, policies concentrated on creating strong ties between central party and government organs in Beijing and the most far-flung of minorities areas. Economic policies were redistributive: revenue flowed out of wealthy provinces and cities into poorer areas, many of them inhabited by minorities. Both economic plans and social policies were centrally planned and transmitted downward. Factories in such places as Shanghai actually took over the manufacture of certain articles in minority styles. Minorities cadres-in-training could study their own cultures at the party-established Central Minorities Institute in Beijing or, slightly later, in branch institutes in provincial capitals. So-called autonomous areas that were granted to minorities were under fairly tight central government supervision. The party took over the role of protector and shaper of minority cultures.

Apart from the Great Leap Forward and Cultural Revolution, minorities retained the right to use their native languages. Those with ambition, however, quickly realized the value of being fluent in the Han language. The party and the institutions it had created were the major channels of social mobility, not the traditional leadership forms that had existed prior to 1949. Han administrators held the preponderance of power even in areas where there were almost no Han, and few troubled themselves to learn local languages despite repeated government admonitions to do so. Those minorities who wished to be included in leading bodies understood the value of being able to communicate with these administrators and their superiors. The educational systems, the economies, and the legal systems of minority areas were controlled by the central government.

By the time Mao died in September 1976, minorities appeared to have acquiesced to the rule of the Communist Party and their inclusion under the jurisdiction of the PRC. Uprisings had occasionally succeeded in winning some concessions, though at considerable human cost to their perpetrators, participants, sympathizers, and their families. Certain concessions notwithstanding, the party and government had made it clear that neither independence nor true autonomy was an option.

Post-Mao Policies

The radically different economic policies instituted by Mao's successor, Deng Xiaoping, had profound consequences for ethnic minority areas, though this was more an indirect result than a conscious design of the new policies. Deng's paramount goal of creating prosperity could best be achieved by investing capital where it had the highest multiplier effect. In general, this meant in coastal cities such as Shanghai and Guangzhou or major river ports like Wuhan. Certain areas such as Shenzhen and Zhuhai received tax breaks and other perquisites designed to draw in foreign capital. None of these were in minorities areas, whose inhabitants were told that they would have to adjust to the market economy: subsidies were replaced with loans. Just as in Han rural areas, minorities received the right to sell their goods on the free market.

The policy of nationalities problems being class problems was officially repudiated, it being explained that Mao had been "misunderstood." Differences between minorities and Han were henceforth to be understood as a function of income inequalities between the two groups. As living standards equalized, tensions would disappear. Overt differences between minorities and Han, such as language, dress, and customs, should not be expected to disappear in the near future, if at all. This went beyond the Mao era's periods of willingness to temporarily accommodate minorities special characteristics and toward a pluralist model of long-term acceptance of these characteristics. To help reduce tensions between Han and non-Han, minorities were exempted to various degrees from the one-child policy imposed on Han. Their children also enjoyed easier access to higher education.

Reform Produces Problems

Various problems arose. With investment capital, both domestic and from foreign businesspeople, flowing into selected enclaves, economic redistribution now made these already relatively prosperous areas still wealthier; minorities areas fell behind. While the new rural policies increased food supplies in minority areas, they also re-established the class inequities the Communist Party said it had come to rectify. Those who were disadvantaged by the reforms felt that the party was breaking faith with the masses. A study of Tibetan herders indicated that the newly prosperous families were precisely those who had prospered under the pre-communist system. Replacing subsidies with loans had disadvantageous results as well, since minorities often did not understand how the loans worked. There was a tendency to borrow too much, make poor investment choices, and then be unable to repay the loans.

The inflation that accompanied burgeoning production in coastal areas proved disproportionately hurtful to minority areas as well. Typically they had been the suppliers of raw materials to the manufacturing areas of the coast. Finished products were then available for purchase at value-added prices. When these prices rose sharply, minorities' sense that they were being exploited by the Han—a feeling that had been present long before the Communist Party ever existed—was reinforced. At one point, the Xinjiang Uygur Autonomous Region actually banned the "import" from other provinces of no less than forty-eight kinds of products including soap, bicycles, and color television sets.[3]

There was famine in Tibet and unrest in Xinjiang. In Tibet, a party policy of forcing people to plant wheat rather than the barley that the local population favored had proved unsuited to the climate. Transport aircraft were sent to evacuate Han. In Xinjiang, Han cadres were quietly withdrawn from the grass roots, a fact not revealed until late May 1998, when the withdrawal was linked to the beginnings of subversive religious activities there.[4] In Yunnan, there were disputes over land and water rights. Minorities' land and rubber trees were illegally appropriated when plantations were established.

Reforming the Reforms

Efforts were made to deal with these problems. Tibetans were again allowed to cultivate barley; state subsidies were increased. Tibet was also exempted from certain taxes. Border minorities in general were encouraged to develop their economies through trade with neighboring countries. Hence, Tibetans began to trade with Nepal and India; Yunnan minorities with Laos, Burma, and Thailand, Xinjiang minorities with the Soviet Union; and Inner Mongolians with the Mongolian People's Republic and the Soviet Union. Tourism to minorities areas began to be encouraged. The government also announced that foreign investment in minorities areas would be welcomed. While realizing that the investment potential was not as great as that in coastal areas, there was a good possibility that foreigners might wish to invest for essentially non-economic reasons. For example, wealthy Saudis or Malaysians might wish to aid their co-religionists in China. Hu Yaobang, on the eve of his appointment as First Party Secretary, made an inspection visit to Yunnan to try to soothe the problems there.

New Problems

Well-meant as these efforts were, there were serious side effects. Borders became more porous. Calls for increased trade, tourism, and foreign investment in minorities areas coincided with an upsurge of fundamentalist sentiments in the Muslim world. Those who came to invest were interested in how their fellow Muslims were treated, and often asked to tour mosques and religious schools. Spies could pose as businesspeople or tourists. Given that few Han administrators in minority areas had learned the local languages, foreign visitors could often converse freely with minorities while their guides remained oblivious to what was being said. Subversive materials, weapons, and explosives could be smuggled in, and letters and tapes alleging or documenting atrocities smuggled out. Yunnan's border trade included an upsurge of traffic in the Golden Triangle's most famous export product: opium.

Dai minorities were impressed with the affluent lifestyles of their fellow Thai who came as tourists to Yunnan. The cultural and economic lure of Bangkok was apparently strong enough that when Thailand's state airline suggested opening a direct route from Chiang Mai to Jinghong, the capital of the Xishuangbanna Dai Autonomous Prefecture, Beijing refused. Investors from the Republic of Korea (ROK) similarly impressed their fellow Koreans in the PRC. Until the authorities began to keep close watch on them, Chinese Korean "tourists" simply disappeared after checking into their Seoul hotel rooms, finding it quite easy to find jobs in the then-booming South Korean economy. Chinese Koreans tried to enter the ROK on undocumented boats as well. ROK police also discovered a thriving marriage-of-convenience market involving elderly ROK males and young Chinese Korean women.

There were also complaints that the policies devised to develop the economies of minority areas primarily benefited the Han residents thereof. This was an especially sore point in Tibet, where the above-mentioned tax exemptions resulted in a flood of Han migrants into the TAR to take advantage of them. Most of the peddlers in the tourist areas of Lhasa were Han from Sichuan. Western guests at the Lhasa Holiday Inn who spoke Tibetan to waitresses wearing traditional Tibetan clothing discovered that the young women were likewise Han.[5] To make matters worse, non-migrant workers brought in under government auspices to work at jobs that included weaving traditional Tibetan carpets received higher wages than did the Tibetans who worked alongside them.[6] The authorities argued that these skilled workers were enhancing economic benefits for all. Tibetans felt that they were being made into second-class citizens in their own country, and that any Han who were brought in were taking jobs away from Tibetans.

Construction workers building pseudo-Dai structures in Jinghong, presumably for the benefit of tourists, were likewise Han migrant workers. In northwest China, Uygurs and Kazakhs complained that Han received preference for better jobs in "their" oilfields and elsewhere. The central government itself admitted that Han migrants had caused ecological damage in Xinjiang through careless use of the land. Environmental damage from Han misuse of the land has been an ongoing complaint among the Mongols of Inner Mongolia, dating at least as far back as the Great Leap Forward. As concerns about the environment in general have grown, so have the complaints.

Whether the benefits of these new economic policies were going primarily to the minorities in minority areas or to the Han in minority areas, the income gap between minority regions and Han China continued to grow. The average industrial and agricultural output in ethnic minority areas had dropped to 47.9 percent of the national average by 1989[7]; nine years and many policy initiatives later, official sources admitted that the gap continued to widen. Only the Guangxi Zhuang Autonomous Region has managed to perform at a level comparable to the rest of Han China. The Zhuang had accommodated well to Han culture long before 1949; Guangxi has also benefited from its geographic location bordering on booming Guangdong province. According to a 1997 report, China's seven worst-performing provinces included all four remaining autonomous areas—Tibet, Ningxia, Xinjiang, and Inner Mongolia—plus three other provinces, Gansu, Guizhou, and Qinghai, with large minority populations.[8] Tibet complained that, once having lifted the poorest of its poor out of poverty, it was difficult to keep them from slipping back. Some areas experienced slight declines in minority education rates.[9]

In any case, and contrary to the assumptions of party policy, narrowing the income and educational gap between minorities and Han will not necessarily end inter-nationality tensions. People who are less focused on sheer survival may have more leisure to indulge their anti-government feelings, and more money to finance the purchase of weapons. Better educational levels may stimulate interest in one's indigenous culture and enhance one's ability to learn more about it. A number of the Inner Mongolian dissidents who were arrested on splittist charges were graduates of the party's own institutes, where they had become interested in going beyond the officially-sanctioned versions of Mongolian culture.

External Factors

While some members of minorities profited from the presence of the outsiders and welcomed them, others felt that the central government was exploiting them on behalf of its desire for more foreign exchange. There were also complaints that the government was perverting and trivializing their culture. Indeed many of the handicrafts marketed as minority-made are not authentic in style and not made by minorities. So-called minority villages, in which foreign visitors are shown how several different minority groups live, have struck outsiders as more like theme parks or human zoos than authentic representations of minority life.[10]

Within the Western world, the 1980s and 1990s also saw increased concern with human rights. Tibet in particular captured the imagination of large numbers of Westerners. Buddhism became the fastest-growing religion in the West, and adherents to its Tibetan variant spanned a range that included eminent scholars and prominent entertainers. The Beijing government pointed out that a Dutch woman who was wounded by Chinese police in their confrontation with Tibetan demonstrators was both active in human rights organizations and had visited Tibet an unusually large number of times; if true, it would bolster the government's argument that she had come with subversive intent. Hollywood produced several films sympathetic to the Tibetan cause, and a U.S. congressman slipped into Tibet disguised as a tourist, later charging that the local culture was being systematically destroyed.

Turkish journalists posing as travel agents visited Xinjiang, photographed the ruins of mosques and Islamic schools, and published their findings in popular magazines. Some tourists were simply tourists, but nonetheless sympathetic to human rights concerns and open to requests that they send in pictures of the Dalai Lama—possession of which is intermittently banned by the Chinese government—and take out documents detailing abuses.

These difficulties were compounded by the disintegration of the Soviet Union and its client states. States governed by ethnic groups with kin in China appeared on the PRC's borders. The Mongolian People's Republic, which had discouraged any "Greater Mongolia" sentiments was replaced by a non-communist republic that found it more difficult to repress such feelings. In addition, there was a revival of interest in Tibetan Buddhism, which had been the religion of most Mongols before communism. This was accompanied by an upsurge of interest in studying the Tibetan language. Despite Chinese protests, the Dalai Lama was invited to Mongolia and warmly received.

Repression Increases

The years 1988 through 1990, while these events were unfolding externally, were particularly difficult for Beijing's relations with its most restive minorities. In June 1988, the Dalai Lama addressed the European Parliament in Strasbourg. There he offered Beijing a compromise under which the PRC would have responsibility for Tibet's foreign policy while the TAR would have a popularly elected legislature and its own legal system. Beijing rejected the proposal, lashing out at the European community for hosting the Dalai Lama and at the Dalai Lama for "internationalizing" a domestic issue.

At this point, the central government appears to have decided to add the "stick" of increased repression to the "carrot" of its post-1979 policy of economic development as a solution to its minority problem. Police and military forces in the TAR were augmented with personnel sent in from outside the region. Monasteries were searched, and persons believed to be sympathetic to the Dalai Lama were arrested. Anti-government demonstrations took place in December. In January, the normally placatory Panchen Lama said publicly that, although there had been progress in Tibet since the communists arrived, it comes at too high a price. Four days later, it was reported that the heretofore healthy fifty-one year old had died of a heart attack. Many assumed he had been killed for speaking out, and there were more protests. Martial law was declared in Lhasa in the spring, and continued for more than a year. During this time, the Dalai Lama was awarded the Nobel Peace Prize.

Also in the spring of 1989, Uygurs and Kazakhs attacked Communist Party headquarters in Urumqi with rocks and steel bars. The publication in Shanghai of a book containing defamatory statements about Islam was the major cause of the protest, though other, ongoing grievances were expressed as well. At the same time, Chinese Muslims (Hui) were causing problems in neighboring Gansu and Qinghai provinces, over other Islam-related issues. Their activities included attacks on rail lines, causing several suspensions in service. A government investigation produced evidence of collusion among Muslim groups in different provinces, as well as foreign support for their activities. A number of Han settlers moved into Xinjiang's border with the former Soviet Union to provide a buffer against movements of minorities back and forth, which provided a further irritant in that area. Major protests occurred in Inner Mongolia as well; these seem to have been influenced by the growth of anti-communist sentiment in neighboring Mongolia. There were sharp crackdowns in all these areas. Inner Mongolia's leadership group was re-organized. Teams investigated monasteries in Tibetans areas and mosques and religious schools in Islamic enclaves. There were many arrests, some for matters that might have been considered relatively trivial a few years before. For example, members of two organizations to promote research into Mongolian culture, both of whom had tried to register themselves legally with the government, were accused of subversive and splittist intentions. In Tibet, people protesting economic problems, which would previously have been tolerated because the issues were not political, were arrested.

Official propaganda stressed that the problems had been caused by a small handful of malcontents who had deceived some others. Most people were happy, and appreciated the many benefits party and government had brought to their previously backward areas. Han and minorities were interdependent: each must help the other for the good of the country as a whole. Although the central government did extract resources from minority areas, it paid a fair price for these materials. Moreover, it also subsidized the economies of many minority areas.

Certain concessions have been made to minorities within the context of these efforts at repression of expressions of discontent. For example, it was revealed that urban renewal plans for Beijing had originally entailed the razing of an area inhabited by migrants from Xinjiang known, appropriately, as Xinjiang Village. The government announced that it had decided to spare the village to avoid offending (or perhaps inciting to riot) its residents.[11] For the same reason, the central government resisted for several years ratifying an agreement between the Xinjiang and Guangdong provinces that would have allowed Guangdong to prosecute Xinjiang natives who ran a highly profitable smuggling operation near Baiyun airport.[12] And the revised criminal law introduced at the March 1997 National People's Congress stated that the author of any publication insulting or discriminating against ethnic minorities could receive a jail term of up to three years. The same law, however, provided for even harsher sentences of up to ten years for persons who "take advantage of national or religious problems to instigate the splitting of the state or undermine the unity of the state."[13]

However, there are differences of opinion between party and government on the one hand and certain members of minorities on the other on what constitutes fostering the development of minority languages, cultures, and traditions, which party and government publicly favor, and undermining the unity of the state and engaging in splittist activities. Clearly, the central leadership reserves for itself the right to make that determination. In practice, it would also seem that cultural development carried on by party and government *on behalf of* minorities is acceptable, whereas cultural development carried out by minorities on their own behalf is not. Ethnic minority culture under the direct control of party and government is celebrated; all other manifestations thereof are regarded with utmost suspicion. In contrast to the marked shifts between accommodationist and assimilationist minorities policies that characterized the early years of the PRC, a model has evolved that is pluralist in form but assimilationist in function.

For example, as plans for a conference on Tibetan literature were being finalized in Beijing[14] and the party was taking credit for rescuing lamaist dances from extinction,[15] one of the last neighborhoods of traditional Tibetan homes in central Lhasa was being destroyed. Several visitors remarked that only the Potala Palace now distinguished the city from one that might be seen anywhere in Han China.[16] In Inner Mongolia, the central government proudly reported that it was refurbishing the mausoleum of Chinggis Khan[17] just weeks after rejecting the appeal of sentences meted out to Mongols who were active in a cultural organization.[18] And the protection of language had limits as well. In an April 1998 speech, Xinjiang's party head, a Han, said that "we say the constitution provides that all nationalities have the freedom to use and develop their spoken and written languages, but this in no way means advocating the use of their own spoken and written languages." He went on to say that since it was impossible to promptly translate many things into minority languages, "it is a very urgent task for cadres of minority nationalities to learn and have a good command of the Chinese language."[19]

To be sure, cultural organizations may have agendas that are more subversive than they seem, choosing to cloak what the Chinese government would call splittist intentions with language classes or dancing lessons. The government charges that Tibetan monasteries have been used to store weapons, Islamic schools for preaching fundamentalist messages, and the Uygur festival *maixilaifu* as a meeting place for subversives.[20] By 1996, the government had declared that religion would have to adapt itself to socialism rather than vice-versa. It underscored this point by rejecting a candidate for the reincarnation of the Panchen Lama who had been approved by the Dalai Lama. The child simply disappeared,[21] and was replaced by a candidate approved by Beijing. The government also said explicitly that areas that were under control of the state and where religion must not intrude included education, family planning, burial arrangements, and the court system.

The central leadership sought as well to enlist the cooperation of border states in curbing dissident activities. This was one aim of the conference with Soviet successor states hosted by President Jiang Zemin in April 1996. More recently, Kyrgyz President Askar Akayev pledged his support against national separatism and religious extremists during a visit to Beijing, as have the heads of Kazakhstan and Tajikistan.[22] Still, there is considerable support within those republics for the cause of Muslims in China, and no leader who depends on the support of his constituents to stay in power can afford to ignore this. The Nepalese government appears to be complying with Chinese wishes regarding dissidents fleeing Tibet, but its border guards are frequently successfully evaded or successfully bribed.

As government repression increases, dissident forces find ways around it. For example, one government effort involved sending work teams into rural areas where they were instructed to set up "joint-defense" teams to ensure public security. It was announced that the teams would apprehend not only dissidents but also those who were found to be harboring a suspect. Both would be punished. Dissidents struck back by assassinating not only those who joined the teams but also their family members. Even religious leaders who appeared to tolerate government supervision, and their family members were targets of assassination.[23]

Government propaganda made much of relatives who vowed to join the teams to avenge the memory of their loved ones, but one doubts that there were large numbers of such volunteers. Xinjiang dissidents in particular moved beyond their province to set off car and bus bombs in Beijing and elsewhere. During times of official celebration or solemnity, including the reversion of Hong Kong in July 1997, the 15th Party Congress in fall 1997 and the 9th National People's Congress in March 1998, Beijing police were alerted to the possibility of violence by minority dissidents. Taxi drivers reported being warned against picking up suspicious-looking passengers, which many interpreted as anyone wearing minority dress or looking non-Han.

Loss of Control At Local Levels

Party and government expressed concerns that there was simply indifference to its wishes at lower levels. There were repeated complaints that primary organizations showed "weak political sensitivity" and had "not exerted themselves in the struggle against national separatism and illegal religious activities."[24] Worse, some officials actively sided with the dissidents. In contravention to the policy that party members should be atheists, they openly practiced their religious beliefs. Tibetan officials maintained lavish shrines in their homes and kept pictures of the Dalai Lama in plain view. A number of cadres whose children attended schools in India run by the Dalai Lama refused a party directive to bring them back.[25]

Officials in Muslim areas proved similarly recalcitrant. In mid-1996 the Xinjiang regional party committee called for "sternly dealing with party members and cadres, especially leading cadres, who continue to be devout religious believers despite repeated education; instill separatist ideas and religious doctrines into young people's minds; publish distorted history; [issue] books or magazines advocating separatism and illegal religious ideas; or make audio or video products propagating such ideas."[26]

These are startling statements, tantamount to admitting that the central government has lost a good deal of control over local levels in these areas. This being the case, it might seem logical to try to blunt the thrust of dissidents as well as accede gracefully to what seems to be happening anyway, by granting true autonomy to so-called autonomous areas. The Dalai Lama has consistently maintained that this would be sufficient for him to return. Some Inner Mongolia dissidents have indicated that this would be acceptable as well.[27]

Genuine Autonomy as a Possible Solution

A law on regional autonomy was in fact devised as part of Deng Xiaoping's reforms. When discussions began on it in 1979, state vice-president Ulanhu, a Mongol leader who had been a party stalwart since the 1920s complained openly that "some Communist Party members hardly sound like Marxists on the question of minority nationalities."[28] The law was duly passed in 1984. Among its salient points was the stipulation that the administrative head of an autonomous region should be a citizen of the nationality or nationalities exercising regional autonomy in the area. The law also gave autonomous areas the power to administer local finances.[29] However, it said nothing about appointing ethnic minorities to leadership positions in the party hierarchy, which is far more crucial. And since the economies of many minority areas depend on state subsidies, which came under the purview of the State Council, there are limits on how financially autonomous they can be.

This analysis assumes that the autonomy law would be enforced. Three years later, Ulanhu was complaining of Han chauvinism blocking its implementation,[30] and criticized higher levels for being unwilling to actually grant autonomy. He took note of minority fears that their areas could be overrun by Han migrants, whom they had no power to keep out.[31] In 1987, a prominent Tibetan with an impeccable record of cooperating with the party termed the lack of implementation of the autonomy law or its partial implementation "quite serious" and accused "some leading cadres" of never even having read it.[32]

Precisely a decade after, Ulanhu's son Buhe, who had essentially inherited his father's status, called for the autonomy law to be not only to be implemented, but extended as well. Obviously choosing his words carefully and expressing himself less bluntly than Ulanhu, Buhe argued that the autonomy law needed to be revised "in line with the market economy," urged that drafting of supplementary legislation, and said that only by rigorously enforcing the rights of autonomy could the unity of the ancestral land be realized. This was widely deconstructed to mean that only a more liberal and better-enforced autonomy law could hope to blunt separatist demands.[33]

Buhe's initiative occurred in the context of reports in the Hong Kong press that a long-standing struggle between the central authorities and the regions had erupted at the March 1997 meeting of the National People's Congress. In internal sessions with central leaders, representatives from ethnic minority areas had purportedly made proposals that could be characterized as "you give us autonomy and we guarantee you stability." Among their demands was that members of ethnic minorities be appointed heads of the Communist Party committees in the areas in which they allegedly exercise autonomy. Others included giving local leaders a greater say on contentious issues such as the numbers of Han Chinese in their areas; the share of profits from the exploitation of the products of their bailiwicks; and the level and disposition of transfer payments and development funds from Beijing.[34] Regional leaders argued that, since the central government was willing to allow Hong Kong, whose population is Han Chinese, a significant degree of autonomy, they should have at least comparable powers. In fact, just the opposite had occurred. Long-standing plans to write more explicit guidelines on the practice of autonomy into law had been postponed as unrest increased in some minority areas.

There has been no indication that the central government is willing to accede to these demands, and it is not difficult to understand why. Even the modest degree of autonomy that minority areas have enjoyed in the years since Mao Zedong's demise has enabled a significant erosion of Beijing's control over those areas. The government fears that granting more autonomy would generate still more demands. What may appear to be reasonable calls for a devolution of decision making may in fact prove the slippery slope toward gradual erosion of all government control and de facto independence. The risks of liberalization would seem to be greater than the risks of continued repression.

It has been argued that allowing Tibet, with its meager resources, forbidding climate, and hostile population to go its own way except for its foreign relations (i.e., to reach an accommodation the Dalai Lama has already proposed) would end a huge financial drain out of the central government treasury as well as eliminate a festering human rights problem. From Beijing's point of view, however, this may appear foolish. Tibet has undoubted strategic value, which must seem all the more important in view of deteriorating relations with India. Western sympathy for Tibet aside, there have been few actual adverse consequences for Beijing as a result of its conduct there. Sustained attention from the international community is unlikely: there will be other causes to attract its attention. The Dalai Lama is sixty; when he dies, Beijing will install a successor, as it has with the Panchen Lama, and take great care with his education.

Moreover, giving Tibet real autonomy would surely stimulate demands for comparable treatment from other areas. Xinjiang has important natural resources in addition to its strategic location, and its dissidents have never indicated that they would be willing to accept anything short of complete independence. Demands for the creation of an East Turkestan Republic hark back to ETRs which had brief existences under the Qing dynasty and the Chinese Republic; they are unlikely to disappear with the current generation of dissidents. Inner Mongolian dissidents have said explicitly that they would be open to the idea of autonomy for the moment, but not necessarily that they would be satisfied with it in the long term.[35]

Beijing would also need to confront the problem of what to do with the Han in minority areas should they gain true autonomy. This would not be a great problem in the Tibet Autonomous Region, but it should be remembered that the TAR is surrounded by autonomous areas belonging to other provinces, but with substantial Tibetan populations. Tibetan dissidents claim these areas as well, and numerous Han live there. In Xinjiang, Han comprise nearly half the population; in Inner Mongolia they are the majority by perhaps six or seven to one.[36] The trend has been to move more Han in to preserve stability and aid in economic development. Minority areas were also designated as receiving areas for at least some of the large numbers of people who have had to be relocated due to the massive Three Gorges dam project.

Conclusions

At present, it does not seem likely that the central government intends to deviate from its current policy of encouraging economic development and suppressing expressions of dissent in ethnic minority areas. It would be unwise for China analysts to extrapolate an increase of ethnic tensions into the indefinite future. Like many other phenomena, they may be cyclical. But, given the difficulties that the Chinese economy faces over the next several years,[37] instability in minority areas is likely to worsen, at least in the short term. The most recent government work reports from Tibet, Xinjiang, and Inner Mongolia are not optimistic, with the word "grim" appearing more than once.[38]

Dissident minorities do not have the strength to force the government to accept their demands for separatism or true autonomy. They will in all likelihood continue to press their demands through remonstrations and demonstrations. But in the absence of some synergism of instabilities generated by demands from Han workers, peasants, and intellectuals, it seems unlikely that they can win anything more than token concessions from the central government.

Notes

1. China's Korean minority, educated under Japanese colonialism, had, and still enjoy, higher levels of education than the Han. The all-but-assimilated Manchu minority has educational standards indistinguishable from the Han. All others are lower. In general, the more rural and the more devout Muslim minorities have lower educational levels. Part of the disparity between Muslim educational levels and those of others is because many, but not all, Muslims are resistant to female education.

2. One notices ambivalence on the matter of culture. Even while official pronouncements were castigating Han culture as the product of a decadent ruling class, it seems to have been regarded as preferable to minorities cultures, perhaps because these were viewed as produced by an even more decadent ruling class with a more primitive culture. Even the impressive embroidery, silverwork, and other artistic traditions of various minorities seem to have been considered as at best quaint curiosities rather than indigenous art forms worthy of admiration.

3. Nicholas Kristof, "In China, Too, Centrifugal Forces Are Growing Stronger," *New York Times*, 26 August 1990, section IV, p. 2.

4. Tseng Shu-wan and Tai Wei, "Xinjiang Launches Immense Infrastructure Projects: In Exclusive Interview with This Newspaper, Wang Lequan Stresses Fight Against Separatism and Social Stability," *Wen Wei Po* (Hong Kong), 26 May 1998, in FBIS-CHI, 26 May 1998, via internet.

5. They complained to the management about what they felt was deliberate deception. On a return visit a year later, the waitresses were Tibetan.

6. This was the equivalent of hardship pay, to compensate for the harsher climate and relative lack of creature comforts in Tibet.

7. "Economic Gap Widens in Minority Areas," *Xinhua*, 25 August 1989, in FBIS-CHI, 28 August 1989, p. 55.

8. Daniel Kwan, "East Still Outshines West for Industry," *South China Morning Post*, 7 April 1997, via internet.

9. Liu Zhenying and Wang Jinfu, "Li Lanqing Emphasizes Great Development of Compulsory Education in Poor Areas," *Xinhua*, 12 May 1998, in FBIS-CHI, 13 May 1998.

10. One of the more recent examples of this appeared in *Far Eastern Economic Review*'s 4 June 1998 issue, p. 40, under the heading "Horror Story." The Liangshan Yi Autonomous Prefecture is planning to provide tourists with a "unique opportunity" to view its "notorious slave system."

11. "Central Authorities Order Various Localities To Handle Nationalities Issues Prudently," *Ming Pao* (Hong Kong), 13 March 1997, p. A 10, in FBIS-CHI, March 15, 1997.

12. Daniel Kwan, "Guangdong, Xinjiang Agree To Combat Smuggling," *South China Morning Post* (Hong Kong), 10 April 1991, p. 10. Guangdong lobbied Beijing

for four years over this agreement; not until the central government became alarmed at the rising drug trade in the area, Sanyuanli, did it finally agree.

13. *Xinhua*, 15 March 1997.

14. Ibid., 20 August 1997.

15. Ibid., 23 August 1997.

16. Hans Vriens, "Lhasa Lost," *Far Eastern Economic Review*, 29 May 1997, pp. 44–45.

17. "$2.8 Million Facelift for Genghis Khan Tomb," *South China Morning Post*, 8 April 1997. No one actually knows where Chinggis Khan is buried; there is also a tomb to him in Mongolia. The Chinese structure was originally built in 1955. Its refurbishment was part of the preparations for the Inner Mongolia Autonomous Region's fiftieth anniversary. It was hoped that the celebrations would attract many tourists. Improvements included the construction of a statue of Chinggis on horseback, a sacrificial altar, a house for sacrifices, and landscaping.

18. *Agence France Presse* (AFP; Hong Kong), 7 February 1997.

19. Wang Lequan "Strive To Build A Contingent of High-Quality Cadres," *Xinjiang Ribao*, 26 April 1998, in FBIS-CHI, 27 May 1998.

20. Luo Wanghao, "Determined Efforts Must Be Made To Eliminate 'Vermin'; Eradicate Poisonous Weeds," *Xinjiang ribao*, 28 July 1997, p. 1, in FBIS-CHI, August 11, 1997.

21. He has been reported as alive and well but under house arrest at an unspecified location. Some reports have put the child in Huairou, outside Beijing, and others in Gansu, where there is a sizeable Tibetan population. The central government's candidate, by contrast, was received by Jiang Zeming in a well-televised ceremony.

22. "Kyrgyz Support over Separatists," *South China Morning Post*, April 29, 1998.

23. "Speech of Amudun Niyaz at a Cadres' Meeting in Ili Prefecture, 19 July 1997," *Xinjiang ribao*, 23 August 1997, pp. 1–2, in FBIS-CHI, 8 September 1997.

24. See, for example, Quan Deyi, "A Basic Project for Safeguarding Xinjiang's Stability," *Xinjiang ribao*, 13 January 1998, in FBIS-CHI, 10 February 1998.

25. Ni Banggui, "Paying Attention to Politics Should Be Closely Linked With Tibet's Reality." *Xizang ribao* (Lhasa), 13 May 1996, p. 4, in FBIS-CHI, June 3, 1996, pp. 35–39.

26. "Regional Discipline Inspection Commission and Regional Supervision Department Call on Discipline Inspection and Supervision Organs Across Xinjiang to Strictly Enforce Political Discipline and Maintain the Stability of the Overall Situation," *Xinjiang ribao*, 22 May 1996, p. 1, in FBIS-CHI, June 7, 1996, pp. 82–84.

27. Nicholas Kristof, "Restlessness Reaches Mongols in China," *New York Times*, 7 July 1992, p. IV 3.

28. Ulanhu, "Address To the Standing Committee of the Politburo," *Xinhua*, 19 June 1979.

29. See "Explanation of Law on Regional Autonomy for the PRC's Minority Nationalities," Beijing, State Council Bulletin no. 13, 30 June 1984, pp. 430–437, in *Joint Publications Research Service: China: Politics and Sociology*, 84–92, 331 December 1984, pp. 1–9.

30. Ulanhu, "The Glorious Course of Regional Autonomy of Minority Nationalities, " *Renmin ribao*, 14 July 1987, pp. 2–3, in FBIS-CHI, 21 July 1987, p. K 13.

31. "Ulanhu Calls for Cadres and the Masses to Study and to Implement the Law on Regional Autonomy for Minority Nationalities," *Renmin ribao*, 30 September 1987, p.1, in FBIS-CHI, 7 October 1987, p. 13. Underscoring Ulanhu's annoyance with this matter, the article had been delivered as a television address the evening before.

32. "Ngapoi Ngawang Jigme Interviewed," *Xinhua*, 6 November 1989, in FBIS-CHI, 8 November 1989, pp. 21–22.

33. See, for example, Bu He, "Legal Construction for Nationalities Essential to Rule of Law," *Qiushi*, 16 April 1997, no. 8, pp. 14–18, in FBIS-CHI, 17 June 1997; Zhang Minhua and Yin Hongdong, "Upholding and Improving the System of Regional Autonomy and Developing Nationality Solidarity: Interview with Buhe, Vice-Chair of the National People's Congress Standing Committee," *Xinhua*, 21 April 1997, in FBIS-CHI, 23 April 1997; for commentary on Buhe's arguments, see Agatha Ngai, "Appeal To Revise Law On Regional Autonomy," *South China Morning Post*, 3 April 1997 and Vivien Pik-kwan Chan, "Legal Push On Ethnic Policy To Improve Unity," *South China Morning Post*, 8 April, 1997, via internet.

34. Willy Wo-lap Lam, "Warlords Make Their Play," *South China Morning Post*, 19 March 1997, via internet.

35. In the words of a 27–year old China-born Mongol who heads a dissident organization based in Ulan Bataar, "the *first* thing we need to get is the freedom to express our grievances…at the *very least*, we need real autonomy…" (emphasis added). Quoted by Nicholas Kristof, *op. cit.*

36. The actual estimate is something like 6.4 to 1. This may be misleading, because a number of Han have re-registered as Mongols to secure the benefits of affirmative action: exemption from the one-child policy, preferential admission to universities, and so forth.

37. Problems include, but are not confined to, how to cope with falling demand for Chinese exports due to the Asian currency crisis; the need to restructure the PRC's economy and particularly the state-owned enterprises, and the creation of 20 million new jobs each year to absorb baby-boomers who are entering the job market.

38. The first quarter growth of GDP in Xinjiang was up a bare 4.2 percent, the third lowest in China after Shaanxi and the Ningxia Hui Autonomous Region; a slowdown in demand for the region's two major exports, oil and cotton ("black gold and white gold") was blamed. Profits of companies fell 32.4 percent and the combined losses of firms rose 89.7 percent. Mark O'Neill, "Urumqi Briefing: Tianshan Debut a Sign of Hope While Xinjiang Struggles To Compete," *South China Morning Post Business Post*, Monday May 18, 1998, via internet. Tibet's 1997 report (i.e., *before* the Asian currency crisis,) was even less inspiring. Of its 2.8 million *yuan* budget, slightly more than half represented a flat subsidy from the central government; additional subsidies were made available for other projects such as schools, border construction, and highway maintenance. Yang Xiaodu, Report to the 5th Session of the 6th Regional People's Congress, 15 May 1997, *Xizang ribao*, 2 June 1997, in FBIS-CHI, 17 July 1997.

11

Chinese Social Trends: Stability or Chaos?

Martin King Whyte

In recent years attempts to analyze and predict political and social trends in the PRC have yielded wildly divergent scenarios. In what might be termed the "stability" scenario, it is noted that China has been much more successful than Russia or Eastern European countries in implementing market reforms while simultaneously raising living standards. The general improvements in people's lives and the many new opportunities for enrichment available are seen as leading to acceptance of the political status quo, or even gratitude. When combined with the political lessons of the 1989 crackdown, these features of the Chinese situation are said to lead most Chinese to have little interest in politics or inclination to take risks to press for political changes. As long as China's leaders remain unified and can keep the engine of economic growth going, according to this scenario, they should be able to maintain the status quo and keep social tensions and conflicts under control.

A very different set of considerations is stressed in what might be termed the "chaos" scenario. This alternative stresses the wrenching and destabilizing impact of the shift from a socialist to a market system. As established ways of doing things and forms of security provided by socialist institutions are undermined, many Chinese struggle to cope and to learn how to operate in the new system. All around them they see reemerging the "social evils" that socialism was supposed to eliminate—foreign ownership, landlordism, prostitution, criminal syndicates, etc.

Inequalities in income and wealth grow rapidly, and the conviction is widely shared that those who are monopolizing the gains are doing so through connections and corruption, rather than due to entrepreneurship, hard work, or great skill. The previous moral orthodoxy provided by Marxism-Leninism-Mao Zedong thought is in shambles, but no alternative moral vision has arisen to fill the vacuum. Increasingly Chinese see their society as characterized by an amoral, man-eat-man struggle, and in this context leaders at all levels are seen as venal and self-serving. Political controls and coercion may keep popular anger hidden much of the time and yield an appearance of political stability, but underneath the surface popular anger remains at high levels, and a variety of incidents and trends may lead to large-scale protests and political crises. In urban areas, in particular, residual hostility stemming from the Tiananmen massacre in 1989 increases the popular anger directed at the CCP. The chaos scenario, then, leads one to see China's leadership as sitting on top of a social volcano that may erupt at any moment.[1]

When confronted with such contradictory assessments of the situation, one is inevitably reminded of the fable of the blind men groping at different extremities of an elephant and trying to figure out what it is. As a sociologist I make no claim to be able to predict the future. However, this chapter will attempt to describe the broader context of the changes in China since 1978 in the hope that this context will help us judge the likelihood that a variety of social trends and tensions will threaten China's political stability. As the reader will see, this assessment will lead to the conclusion that there is considerable truth to the trends and dynamics stressed by both the "stability" and "chaos" scenarios, although not necessarily to the conclusions drawn from them. In other words, this analysis should lead to a greater understanding of the shape of the Chinese social elephant, but not necessarily to an ability to confidently predict whether that elephant will remain passive or go on a rampage.

Transformed State-Society Relations

Conventional wisdom holds that Deng Xiaoping and his colleagues presided over an attempt to reform the Chinese economy while preventing changes in the PRC's party-dominated political institutions. However, even cursory examination reveals that the major changes that have swept China since 1978 have not been confined to the economic realm. China is a very different society politically (as well as culturally and otherwise) than it was at the time of Mao's death, and the fundamental changes that have occurred in the nature of state-society relations increase the difficulty of ruling the world's most populous society. In order to understand these changes it is necessary to briefly review the nature of the political and social order of the late-Mao era.

While China at the end of the Mao era is sometimes characterized as an egalitarian socialist order, the reality was more like a rigid, hierarchical form of feudalism with a strong admixture of Confucian statecraft. Individuals and families were either born into (in the case of rural communes) or bureaucratically allocated to (in the case of urban work units) relatively closed organizational cells where they served at the pleasure of the state. There was little in the way of free movement of people and information across the organizational boundaries of this cellular system. While there were strenuous efforts to provide social security and relatively egalitarian distribution of income and social services within each cell, the cells themselves were arranged in a vast and very unequal hierarchy. Access to income, opportunities, information, and everything else varied sharply depending upon where you were in the bureaucratic system. The social world of those in advantaged cells (e.g., in resource-rich central work units located in urban areas) was profoundly different from those at the bottom of the system of bureaucratic ranks and caste-like groups (e.g., individuals in poor villages in the hinterlands, members of political pariah groups).

Authority over this feudal-like hierarchy rested in the CCP and ultimately in its leader, Mao Zedong. The CCP used its control over information and communications to ensure that no rival ideas could compete with the official Marxist-Leninist-Maoist orthodoxy. Extraordinary efforts were regularly made to indoctrinate all citizens into this faith and to use political study, criticism rituals, campaigns, and coercion to ensure that critical and alternative viewpoints could not be spread and threaten faith in the official orthodoxy.[2] That orthodoxy stressed themes such as individual and group sacrifice in the pursuit of the distant goals of socialism and communism, the constancy of class struggle, and veneration of Mao Zedong. Experiences of life in Maoist China produced personal hardship and family tragedies for many. However, any tendency to translate such experiences into shared grievances against the system, the CCP, and Mao was generally squelched by the quasi-totalitarian nature of CCP control over the social order and communications. No general public opinion could emerge within this social order, and individuals who harbored doubts or hostility toward Mao and the CCP tended to feel that they were isolated and out of step with the vast masses of enthusiastic citizens around them, comrades who were devotedly building socialism under the wise leadership of Mao. Getting ahead or just getting by depended primarily on currying favor with the bureaucratic gatekeepers in charge of your cell, rather than on any attempt to escape from your lot or to join with others to challenge the system.[3]

When the late-Mao social and political order is described in these shorthand terms, it immediately becomes apparent that this order has since been transformed in multiple and fundamental ways. Those changes began to occur already during the Cultural Revolution, and not simply after 1978. Although the Cultural Revolution appeared at times to be the zenith of totalitarian controls over the masses, the reality was more complex. The entire edifice of Party organizational controls and regular indoctrination of the masses fell apart for several years (roughly from mid-1966 until at least 1969), as did cellular controls on the movement of people and information. During periods of Cultural Revolution chaos, large numbers of people were on the move across the face of China (particularly, but not exclusively, young people). They had unprecedented opportunities to observe their society directly and to talk to individuals from other locales and walks of life without the normal supervision and controls of their unit's organizational discipline. This period of extended personal autonomy had a profound impact on the outlooks of many Chinese citizens, especially as their observations of rural poverty, elite arrogance and corruption, and violence contrasted sharply with the faiths they had absorbed prior to the Cultural Revolution. Even though Mao and his colleagues tried to revive the CCP and its systems of political controls and indoctrination after 1969, the damage proved irreparable. Many Chinese citizens by the early 1970s held an altered and darker picture of the nature of their social order, even though they knew that it was still dangerous to share this view with others.

The post-Mao changes ended this attempt to restore the former system of totalitarian control over people and ideas and fundamentally altered the nature of state-society relations. As noted earlier, there were multiple aspects of this transformation. The combination of the repudiation of the Cultural Revolution (and, by implication, of Mao's leadership) and the shift from a system of bureaucratic allocation to market distribution further undermined faith in the previous Marxist-Leninist-

Mao Zedong Thought orthodoxy. The open door policy also brought into China vast infusions of alternative ideas and cultural forms from which Chinese citizens had previously been isolated. At the same time the belief that China was at the vanguard of the advance toward a better socialist future was replaced by official recognition that China was falling behind and needed to do whatever was necessary to avoid being left in the dust by more rapidly developing countries in Asia. The relaxation of CCP controls over acceptable styles of behavior, dress, culture, religion, and thinking combined with mass rehabilitations of victims of earlier campaigns had similar effects. These changes encouraged pluralism of thought and behavior and undermined any remaining view that there was only one proper, "proletarian" way for everyone to think and behave. The cellular walls of China's bureaucratic hierarchy also began to decay, with large scale migration occurring and a growing opportunity (or necessity) for individuals to leave the eroding security of their own units to compete in the new market environment. By the 1990s the socialist "social contract" had been fundamentally weakened, with security of employment, compensation, housing, health care, education, and other basics of life increasingly threatened, requiring individual and family decisions and investments in place of bureaucratic provision.

There are a variety of formulations that have been used to characterize the changes in the Chinese political economy resulting from China's reforms. For example, analysts describe the shift of China from a totalitarian to an authoritarian system, from bureaucratic allocation to market distribution, and from a socialist social contract to a new social contract based upon competition for individual and family enrichment. Whatever the particular rubric favored, there is general consensus that the political atmosphere in the PRC has been dramatically altered. Individuals and families have substantially more autonomy in most areas of their personal lives than they had in the Mao era, with their human rights less systematically violated.[4] They are exposed to a variety of forms of culture, ideas, and values, rather than to the monochromatic proletarian straight-jacket of the late Mao era. Public opinion has emerged as a political force in contemporary China, with the CCP hard-pressed to counter attitudes and opinions that differ from the official line. Individuals no longer feel surrounded by zealous activists who will denounce them if they make a comment that deviates from the approved orthodoxy. Instead in some instances remaining "true believers" may feel isolated in the midst of increasingly critical and cynical colleagues. Political jokes at the expense of China's leaders which would have led to personal disaster in the late-Mao era are now widely shared and enjoyed. I imagine Jiang Zemin, Li Peng, and their colleagues feeling they suffer from a Chinese version of the "Rodney Dangerfield" syndrome—no matter what they do, they "don't get no respect." Clearly this is not a system which has maintained its political system intact while changing its economy.[5]

One might argue that in many respects the changes that have occurred in China since the 1970s, when taken as a whole, can be interpreted as indicating that the country is becoming a more "normal" society after a decidedly abnormal, totalitarian interlude during Mao's rule. And in any normal society, one might generalize, having vibrant and volatile public opinion trends and a healthy disrespect for political leaders should not pose a particular threat to the stability of the system. Indeed, it is a commonplace of political analysis that political systems which allow people to express their views and even their anger and thus provide "safety valves" for such sentiments are likely to be more stable than political systems which keep such feelings bottled up.

However, there are several problems with using this sort of "return to normalcy" argument to favor the "stability" over the "chaos" scenario. First, both China's imperial and socialist histories and the partial nature of the political changes since 1978 make the "safety valve" metaphor problematic. As Frank Parkin observed long ago in a related context, one of the virtues of a fully developed capitalistic system is that individual discontent tends to be vented in multiple directions—against rivals, one's own failings, the vagaries of the market, or fate, for example—and not primarily against the state. However, in a state socialist or other redistributive system, there is a very strong tendency for the state to be either credited or blamed for what happens in people's lives.[6] Market reforms may have been calculated by Deng Xiaoping and his colleagues to eventually lessen the tendency of popular feelings to be focused on the state, but at present the state's hand in the PRC is very far from being "invisible." Thus Jiang Zemin and his colleagues cannot take much comfort in the hope that their citizens will express their discontents in various and politically unthreatening ways. At present the leadership will continue to have good reason to fear the tendency for such popular feelings to be readily converted into anger at the system and the CCP itself.

A related reason why the expression of popular discontent cannot be presumed by the CCP to be normal and non-threatening stems from the party's efforts to maintain its dominant organizational role in the altered political atmosphere of contemporary China. With intermediate associations and institutions remaining weak, hobbled by CCP supervision, or absent, the population may often feel that there are few or no viable channels through which their grievances and demands for redress may be fairly expressed and acted upon. Even though some aspects of the reforms, such as legal institutionalization and experiments with labor arbitration, are designed to overcome this problem, China's reality at present is one in which procedures for dealing with popular grievances remain weak and ad hoc. And as Samuel Huntington observed long ago, political systems which arouse high popular expectations without developing effective institutional mechanisms for handling such feelings within the system are asking for trouble.[7]

To sum up, the changes in China since the Mao era have produced a major alteration in the relationship between the CCP and the population. While elements of these changes may eventually help to promote political stability, at the moment there remains a problematic situation. The CCP can no longer so effectively control mass sentiments and their public expression, and indeed a major reason for this change is that in the Deng era the CCP has not normally tried to do so. However, when popular discontent increases and particularly when it gets translated into mass demonstrations, the CCP tends to feel threatened but at the same time to lack effective mechanisms for responding. The CCP's response is often to fall back on its repertoire of political rituals from the Mao era—for example, by declaring the actions in question a threat to the system, launching a political campaign, and using coercion to eliminate the leaders of such demonstrations while scaring any followers. (Witness the "three speaks" campaign aimed at elites and the over-the-top assault on the *Falun Gong* sect launched in 1999.) Given the wholesale loss of credibility of the ideological symbols used by the CCP to justify such responses, as well as the general popular distaste for the political rituals of the Mao era, these habitual regime responses are not effective ways to rebuild respect for the CCP and its leaders.

The immediately preceding comments might be interpreted as leading to a prediction that favors the "chaos" rather than the "stability" scenario. However, such a conclusion would be premature and oversimplified. My comments to this point indicate that I agree with the portions of the "chaos" scenario that imply that many Chinese individuals and groups are suspicious, cynical, and angry about recent trends. As a result we can expect to see China's leaders at all levels struggling in the years ahead to deal with actual and potential mass contentiousness and fearful of the potential for "chaos." However, evidence on mass movements and collective action around the world indicates that it takes much more than grass roots discontent and anger to produce social movements that can threaten a nation's political stability. Translating popular resentments into serious threats to the system requires a large number of intervening conditions to be present. A listing of the conditions for such a mobilization might include the following:

- grass-roots anger, discontent, and alienation
- the opportunity to broadly share such sentiments with others
- structures promoting social solidarity among the aggrieved
- resources (time, financial, organizational, etc.) to use to pursue the interests of the aggrieved and act on their demands
- sufficient autonomy to be able to resist official dependency and blandishments
- effective leadership willing to take substantial risks to further group demands
- a set of ideas, demands, and moral claims with broad mass appeal beyond the aggrieved group
- opportunities to forge alliances with and recruit support from other groups
- conditions that direct popular anger upward against the central state and its leaders and undermine their legitimacy
- weaknesses or constraints within the state leadership which prevent a unified and effective response and/or which lead potential demonstrators to feel they will receive support or even immunity from coercion from factions within the elite.[8]

Given this laundry list of preconditions, we may conclude that if China remains politically stable in the future, this could be due to some combination of popular satisfaction, passivity, and fear, as the "stability" scenario implies. However, it could instead be due to the regime's skill and/or luck in squelching the many expected grass roots conflicts and protests that occur before they escalate into forms that threaten the system.

China's Current Social Tensions

With these comments as a background, we move into more speculative terrain. The remainder of this chapter will be devoted to brief consideration of a variety of current sources of social tension and conflict in Chinese society, with some thoughts about which are likely to prove most serious or difficult to keep from escalating into a challenge to regime stability. Among those social tensions and disgruntled groups most often listed as potential threats to the system are the following:

- Ethnic tensions between minorities and Han Chinese.
- Resentments of those in China's interior against the favored coastal regions.
- Anger of Chinese peasants against their low status and persistent mistreatment.
- Discontented and rootless members of China's "floating population."
- Hostility of SOE workers, laid-off workers, and pensioners at their loss of status, benefits, and security.
- Alienation of students and intellectuals.
- Alternative faiths and sects à la *Falun Gong*.

What are the conditions likely to make each of these potential sources of tension either a manageable or a very serious threat to China's political stability?

Ethnic tensions: The general relaxation of political controls in the post-Mao period reviewed earlier in this paper has allowed a significant resurgence of cultural and religious activity among China's non-sinicized minority nationalities. Particularly in Tibet and in Xinjiang, these trends have led to recurrent protests and challenges to Chinese rule, and to the mobilization of state coercion and controls in response. Several conditions seem likely to make these problems continue, including increased Han migration into minority regions and greater awareness of, and contacts with, ethnic and religious brethren outside China's borders. However, the peripheral location of the most serious conflicts and the lack of any signs of substantial support among Han Chinese for minority rights make it seem unlikely that these tensions could be translated into a general threat to China's political stability.[9]

Regional Inequality and Resentments from China's Interior: It seems quite clear that state policy and economic development trends since 1978 have further exacerbated already large disparities in income and living conditions between interior regions and provinces and favored coastal locations. A number of Chinese political figures have worried aloud that if nothing is done to redress these growing disparities they will threaten China's stability. However, this seems quite unlikely. Provinces and regions are large and amorphous units that do not lend themselves to strong popular attachments and protest mobilizations. Furthermore, the implied outcome of this kind of destabilization—a fragmentation of the Chinese state into component provinces or other subunits—would only compound the disadvantages of those presently living in interior regions. Unless other considerations argue for the benefits of separation (as with Tibet and Xinjiang), regional disparity trends are likely to lead instead to a variety of efforts by those in the interior to get a better share of the pie of a unified China—through changes in state policy, economic concessions, migration, etc.[10]

Angry Peasants: There are lots of signs that many in the Chinese countryside are angry about their lot and increasingly likely to become contentious. There are a variety of reasons for such sentiments. After being the prime beneficiaries of China's reforms in the early 1980s, China's peasants have increasingly been losing out compared to urbanites. As a result, the gap between average rural and urban incomes has widened since the mid-1980s to levels that are higher than they were in 1978 and unusually large compared to other developing societies.[11] Chinese peasants also bear the brunt of an extraordinarily coercive state-mandated family planning system that makes it very difficult for millions of families to realize cherished fertility goals. Many peasants find that they are at the mercy of local officials who regularly impose extra taxes and fees to support favored projects and blatantly ignore state efforts to outlaw such "excess burdens." Although they are freer than in the Mao era to move around and seek economic opportunities in the cities and elsewhere, the maintenance of the household registration system keeps most peasants confined to a lower caste position, subject to discrimination and mistreatment compared to registered residents of the locales to which they move.

These kinds of problems have produced an upsurge of protest movements across the face of rural China in the 1990s, some of them quite large in scale.[12] Given the fact that the CCP came to power on the basis of a rural revolution, again some analysts within China have seen peasant anger as a serious threat to the system. However, there are a number of reasons for skepticism about such analyses. First, whatever the modest weakening of the power of China's central authority in the reform era, conditions today are far different from those in the 1920s and 1930s, making the establishment of a rural "base area" of protest against the CCP seem quite unlikely. As with regions and provinces, it also seems quite doubtful that rural residents identify strongly with other peasants and feel hatred for urbanites *in general*. Most rural protests seem concerned with much more parochial violations of expected treatment of residents of particular locales due to the actions of local officials at one level or another. To date the authorities have been able, through a combination of concessions and coercion, to prevent such local contentiousness from translating into broader rural protest movements.[13] China's rural residents may not be Marx's "sackful of potatoes," and their growing sophistication and knowledge of the system in which they live makes them increasingly vigorous defenders of their rights, rather than passive tools of their leaders.[14] However, there is little reason to think that recurring protest activity at the grass roots in rural China cannot be dealt with at that level without escalating into a regime-threatening protest movement.

The Floating Population: China's reforms have loosened the feudalistic bonds that tied China's rural residents to their villages, and as a result large numbers of migrants have flooded into China's cities. At any one time it is estimated that there are 80–100 million such members of the "floating population," and favored cities are awash in the resulting human tide. A recent count in Peking, for instance, led to an estimate that that city contained 3 million "floaters" in addition to its roughly 12 million regular urban residents.[15] Many "floaters" manage to find short- or longer-term jobs, but even so they retain the stigma of their rural registration, ineligible for many of the benefits that urbanites receive, and they are often feared and looked down upon by the city's permanent residents.[16] Their marginal connection to the urban system is often seen as making them less likely to play by the official rules, and they are often blamed for the upsurge in serious crimes in cities in recent years.

However, in this case as well there are reasons to doubt that China's floating population will become a serious threat to the system. This doubt is informed by research on squatters and migrants in other developing countries. Fears of migrants as a source of social and political disorder are common, but instances in which they mobilize to challenge the state are extremely rare. Generally speaking, migrants lack many of the structural conditions mentioned above that might translate their resentments into an effective political movement. They come voluntarily in pursuit of advantages and generally stay only when they are successful in this pursuit; their frame of reference tends to be kinsmen back in their village rather than favored urban residents or fellow migrants; they often live dispersed among others with whom they are in competition; they lack the social space, resources, and leaders to effectively mobilize; and so forth. All of these considerations make it seem likely that China's urban migrants are more a source of stability than of instability.[17]

SOE Workers, Laid-Off Workers, and Pensioners: It is common to observe that, even though China's proletarians were never the "masters of the state" that Marxism proclaimed, within the bureaucratic structure of Mao-era China they were fairly well treated. They generally had relative incomes, job security, and fringe benefit coverage that workers in other developing countries could only envy. It is also widely recognized that these advantages have been a primary target of China's reforms, particularly in the 1990s. With large proportions of SOEs operating at a loss and under great pressure to cut costs and downsize, millions of long-time SOE employees have been laid off. Even those who remain at work are often subject to an increasingly draconian industrial regime of rules, fines, and close supervision reminiscent of "scientific management" in early capitalism in the West.[18] Furthermore, many of the subsidies and benefits that they formerly received have been weakened or eliminated, forcing them to pay much more of the cost of housing, medical care, schooling, and other necessities than in the past. Some hard-pressed firms are not able to meet their payrolls or pay the pensions of their retirees, actions that often spawn protests by workers and pensioners, who consider that long-standing commitments are being violated. As present and former SOE workers see the benefits they enjoyed under socialism being whittled away, all around them they can see new beneficiaries of the reforms—for example, private entrepreneurs, foreigners, rural migrants, and a "new class" of officials-turned-business executives. Given these trends it is understandable that worker protests have escalated in recent years, and that fear of worker protests is often seen as a primary obstacle to a more thorough reform of the SOE system.

In this instance the potential for serious challenges from China's SOE workers cannot be dismissed out of hand. There are several structural features of the workers' situation that are conducive to mobilization of worker protest movements. For example, SOE workers remain highly concentrated in relatively large units that long operated as highly integrated "urban villages." The potential for solidarity and sharing of grievances within this sort of structure seems particularly high. The potential for leaders of organized protests to emerge among people who have lived and worked alongside each other for decades also seems considerable. Anger over promises not kept, benefits withdrawn, and jobs lost seems likely to be more politically dangerous than the sort of envy at the more rapid improvement enjoyed by others that is characteristic of many other groups in China today. Furthermore, in this case the tendency to blame the state as the initiator of SOE reforms, rather than oneself, rivals, or local managers, seems relatively great.

However, as of the end of the 1990s large scale layoffs and other problems of SOE workers had not been converted into serious challenges to state authority, and it is reasonable to ask why not. Several other features of the situation of workers seem to counterbalance the tendencies just enumerated, and thus to preserve the status quo. First, the writing has been on the wall for SOE workers since the mid-1980s, so that the loss of their privileges does not come as a shock. Their looming difficulties presumably induced many ambitious and dissatisfied SOE workers to find new employment elsewhere, whether directly from their SOE jobs or after having been laid off. The existence of this "exit" option makes life within an SOE less onerous than in the Mao era, and the selective nature of the exit flow probably acts to insure that those who remain tend to be individuals who are relatively grateful for retaining their dented iron rice bowls and concerned about how they will fare if they lose the remaining pay and benefits. In other words, it seems likely that individuals who are potential militants for workers rights are also more likely than others to leave in pursuit of better opportunities elsewhere.

The fact that most SOE downsizing has taken the form of layoffs rather than outright terminations is also a factor. Those who are laid off continue to receive some pay and often remain in unit-supplied housing as well, benefits that they may fear losing if they rock the boat. The fact that at least until recently China's buoyant economy has provided new job opportunities for many of those laid off, sometimes without jeopardizing the subsistence pay and benefits they receive from their SOE former employer, again seems likely to reduce the potential for worker unrest to escalate into serious challenges. We must also take into account the regime's extraordinary vigilance against any sign of autonomous organizing among workers to advance proletarian claims. The paranoia of China's leaders about the dangers of a Polish-style "Chinese Solidarity" movement makes any effort to mount a worker challenge against the state extraordinarily risky.

Another stabilizing factor is that to date most worker protests seem to have been directed at immediate managements and sometimes at local officials as well, and not upward against the central leadership. There are a variety of possible reasons for this myopic state of affairs.[19] In part what may be operating is a perception that higher levels of the state, while ultimately the inspiration of the reforms that are whittling away worker rights and benefits, are paradoxically also the main source of potential protection against overly aggressive or arbitrary SOE managements. In other words, when a reformist manager implements a threatening new practice that workers want to challenge, their primary recourse is to do such things as stage a sit-in outside local or higher government offices to demand that their grievances be heard. One common response to such protests is for besieged officials to pressure the SOE managers involved to work out concessions in order to restore order, with the state perhaps providing new funding to facilitate such concessions. To the extent that this process recurs, the state may be able to burnish its image as a protector of worker rights, rather than as the ogre who pulled the rug out from under the workers.[20]

A final consideration is that many SOE workers and pensioners may accept the justifications the regime provides for its reforms. China's proletarians are only too aware of how inefficient and unproductive SOEs were in the late-Mao era. Even if they resent the threats the reforms pose to their own livelihoods and work habits, they may nonetheless accept the state's claim that radical SOE reform is necessary in order for China to compete economically. If the legitimacy of such claims is accepted, then worker anger will be directed at those who are seen as unfairly implementing the reforms, not at the central state which launched them. To the extent that this is the case, worker anger as a result of SOE reforms is not likely to translate into a serious challenge to the state.

Alienated Students and Intellectuals: Students and intellectuals have been leading participants in the major demonstrations and crises that have shaken post-1949 China, ranging from the 100 Flowers Campaign of 1956–57 to the Tiananmen demonstrations in 1989. Student protest activity of course has a much longer history in modern China.[21] It is also a commonplace of research on mass movements elsewhere (as well as of Marxist theory) that other groups in society rarely mobilize beyond parochial concerns unless allied with or led by students and intellectuals. For a variety of reasons, then, it is logical to look to China's intellectual elite when contemplating the prospects for stability or chaos in that society.

There are a variety of considerations that are likely to sustain high levels of alienation among China's students and intellectuals. Although some of the major criticisms of the regime raised in 1989 were not so important a decade later—inflation, for example (deflation was more of a danger)—others continue to generate discontent. Corruption continues to be pervasive, with the official campaigns launched against this evil considered highly selective and ineffective. The shopworn socialist slogans and rituals that the regime tries to use to legitimize its programs are widely rejected, and the absence of an alternative moral vision is particularly troubling to the inheritors of China's *literati* tradition. There is also the legacy of the events of 1989, which convinced some members of China's intellectual elite that the regime was so repugnant that it could not be reformed.

Although these considerations indicate that a reservoir of alienation among many students and intellectuals will remain a threat to China's leadership in the years ahead, other developments may make another large scale student uprising less likely. Several features of student life have changed in ways that may reduce the potential for student activism somewhat. University enrollments have expanded substantially in the last decade, a trend that may dilute the likelihood of college students seeing themselves as a deserving elite. The system of bureaucratic assignment to jobs after graduation, which still dominated in 1989 despite official promotion of individual competition for employment opportunities, has for the most part collapsed. Thus students are likely to feel that now they have much more control over their own professional futures, and are less subject to the arbitrariness and favoritism of university bureaucrats. In addition, the authorities are much more vigilant and even paranoid in trying to nip in the bud any early signs of revived campus activism. Regular threats and the annual spring "lockdown" of Beijing area campuses indicate that any future student-led demonstrations will have much more difficulty building up the kind of momentum and support that they received in 1989. The sense of partial immunity to potential regime coercion that helped embolden student protestors in 1989 also is no longer present.

In regard to intellectuals in general, both official policies and economic trends have to a considerable degree altered the situation of the late-1980s, when the rewards of the reforms seemed to be passing them by. Both state-sponsored wage increases for intellectuals and the rapid growth of new high technology employment opportunities in the 1990s have substantially eliminated the situation in which returns to education were abnormally low in late Mao-era and early reform-era PRC.[22] Now once again China's knowledge workers can have some confidence that excelling in school and at work will lead to economic as well as spiritual rewards. Insofar as the hypocrisy of the gap between meritocratic slogans and China's residual bureaucratic/virtuocratic reality was a factor in student and intellectual anger in 1989, this should be less of a factor in the future. In sum, while past history makes it dangerous to discount the potential for a student-led mass movement in the future, on balance this potential source of regime instability also appears somewhat more manageable than in the past.

Alternative faiths and sects: The discussion to this point has focused on a fairly conventional set of potentially aggrieved social groups and has involved a sociological analysis of the forces likely to promote or counteract the tendency of these groups to mobilize to redress grievances. The challenge presented to the regime in 1999 by *Falun Gong* alerts us to the need to consider alternative sources of challenge to regime stability.[23] Although we do not yet have very much research on the membership and organization of this *Qigong* sect, its reported millions of members span regions and social groups, rather than representing a well defined social constituency.[24] There appears to be a tendency for the members to be middle-aged or older and to represent a variety of occupations in urban areas (including party cadres) more than rural China, but still it is the absence of a common social origin that is notable. The sect's members are united not by common social origins, but by their mode of response to China's current moral vacuum. They have found new meaning and moral guidance in an eclectic mixture of *Qigong* rituals and Buddhist and Daoist practices devised by sect founder Li Hongzhi, and in the discipline and solidarity they find among fellow believers in this new (but in some ways very old) faith.

There are several good reasons for China's leaders to be concerned about the challenge posed by *Falun Gong*. They were taken completely by surprise by the 10,000 or so highly disciplined *Falun Gong* members who staged a sit-in outside Zhongnanhai in April 1999. They were presumably very dismayed to discover that their long-standing and vigorous efforts to prevent the formation of any autonomous organizations in China had failed to halt the rise of a movement claiming millions of members nationwide. The awareness that state restrictions on the Internet did not prevent this sect from using new communications technologies to mobilize members to confront the authorities must be particularly worrisome. Knowledge of the key role played by alternative faiths and charismatic leaders in movements that shook or overthrew earlier Chinese dynasties (Li Hongzhi as Hong Xiuquan?) must compound these worries. The dispersed and diverse nature of the membership and the apparent strength of their alternative beliefs seem to make them immune to the kinds of carrots and sticks the regime uses to deal with dissatisfied workers, peasants, or students.

Despite these ominous indicators, there are reasons to question how much of a threat to regime stability this movement can or will pose. Its leader is living in exile in New York, and even with the aid of the Internet, it is not clear how well the movement can respond to regime coercion without its charismatic leader on site to lead the charge. The main thrust of *Falun Gong* activities seems to revolve around personal salvation rather than alternative social and political programs for China. Thus members may "tune out" the political and commercial messages of the society around them without challenging them directly (although that could change as a result of the official suppression campaign). There were no signs as of 1999 that *Falun Gong* had tried to link up with aggrieved peasants, workers, or other groups, a development that would make them much more threatening. Although the movement is very large, at the same time it is also basically a sectarian movement in which you have to believe in order to join and participate. This factor cuts off large and influential parts of China's population, including many young people, Westernized intellectuals, and even supporters of rival *Qigong* masters. In short, the regime seems to have overreacted in claiming that *Falun Gong* represents a serious political threat to the system. Nonetheless, the continuing moral vacuum produced by the collapse of beliefs in Marxism and socialism provides fertile ground for new faiths to arise in China, and if such faiths develop political and social agendas and embed themselves in aggrieved social groups, they could pose serious challenges to the regime.

Conclusions

This survey of potential threats to system stability in China is obviously not exhaustive. One can think of a number of other possible sources of instability—for example, from a military angry about its loss of status and forced divestiture of lucrative business assets, or from diehard Marxist intellectuals attempting to appeal to workers and peasants. Given our inability to anticipate the events of 1989 and the rise of *Falun Gong*, the possibility of new and unforeseen groups and movements mounting a challenge to China's leaders cannot be discounted. However, given this major caveat, the analysis presented here suggests several primary conclusions.

- We can expect a high level of contentiousness and conflict to persist in China in the future, with the regime unable to take the support of large portions of the population for granted.
- The remaining weaknesses of the institutional mechanisms for dealing with popular grievances and mobilized discontent are likely to produce crude and coercive regime responses in some instances, leading to continuing human rights abuses.
- Despite this turbulence, there is no particular group or grievance that appears very likely to pose a fundamental challenge to the leadership in the next few years. If this conclusion is correct, the same kind of muddling through and putting out local "forest fires" erupting from society that has characterized the last few years may continue. In other words, stability of a sort is a reasonable possibility.
- However, stability seems an odd and quite inappropriate term to use for the scenario envisioned here. Terms such as "rocky stability" or "stable unrest" seem closer to the mark.[25] In retrospect, casting the discussion in terms of "stability" versus "chaos" seems misleading and simplistic. One might better conceive of a continuum ranging from a very orderly stability to a revolutionary challenge to the regime. On such a continuum, the analysis here suggests, the most likely prospect for the immediate future is closer to the "chaos" end of the scale, with a variety of kinds of popular turmoil repeatedly testing but not necessarily defeating the leadership's ability to maintain control.
- For the present "rocky stability" to persist depends upon several conditions that, as others have observed, may be difficult to preserve. Economic conditions must continue to generate many new opportunities and jobs without producing spiraling inflation; the leadership must maintain internal unity and avoid splits over how to deal with social eruptions; they must try to ensure that local protests are dealt with quickly and effectively without escalating and allowing alliances to be formed with other aggrieved groups;

and the elite must be willing and able to use substantial coercion to quell protests that escape such initial control efforts.[26]

- Should these conditions not persist, the level of contentiousness and alienation present in Chinese society is such that future social disturbances could escalate into regime-threatening movements. In other words, even though what I have called "rocky stability" appears most likely under present circumstances, in years ahead a movement further down the continuum toward "chaos" is by no means a remote possibility.
- If the present analysis is accurate, the challenges for U.S. policy are considerable. While we have a strong interest in China's stability, the ways in which this stability is maintained are likely to include measures that we find highly unpalatable. Although we may be able to provide some forms of assistance that will lessen the chances of social instability—such as through fostering continued legal reform and further development of institutional mechanisms for expressing and resolving grievances—our actions generally will be quite peripheral to the sorts of social dynamics dealt with here. The United States will also continue to face the dilemma of how much support and face to provide to leaders who, however vital they may be to avoiding chaos, represent an outmoded and failed social movement of an earlier era.

Notes

1. For an informative journalistic version of the "chaos" viewpoint, see James Miles, *The Legacy of Tiananmen: China in Disarray*, Ann Arbor: University of Michigan Press, 1997.

2. See the discussion in my book *Small Groups and Political Rituals in China*, Berkeley: University of California Press, 1974.

3. These comments are inspired by the framework for analyzing subordinate orientations and actions introduced by Albert Hirschman in his book *Exit, Voice, and Loyalty*, Cambridge: Harvard University Press, 1972. That scheme helped inspire a number of studies of organized dependency in Mao-era China. See, in particular, Gail Henderson and Myron Cohen, *A Chinese Hospital*, New Haven: Yale University Press, 1984; Andrew Walder, *Communist Neo-Traditionalism*, Berkeley: University of California Press, 1986.

4. One clear exception to this generalization is in the realm of family planning. See my article, "Human Rights Trends and Coercive Family Planning in the PRC," *Issues and Studies*, 1998, 34: 1–29.

5. Obviously not everything has changed. The CCP still clings to its exclusive role at the center of the political system and tries to prevent any autonomous orga-

nizations from emerging and becoming influential. Furthermore, there are clearly limits to what kinds of political views can be expressed and how, with individuals and groups which go beyond those limits getting into serious political trouble. However, on balance the boundaries of tolerated attitudes and expression have widened considerably since Mao's death.

6. See Frank Parkin, *Marxism and Class Theory: A Bourgeois Critique*, London: Tavistock, 1979.

7. Samuel Huntington, *Political Order in Changing Societies*, New Haven: Yale University Press, 1968.

8. The social science literature on the preconditions for regime-threatening mass movements is extensive. See, for example, Charles Tilly, *From Mobilization to Revolution*, Reading, MA: Addison-Wesley, 1978; Theda Skocpol, *States and Social Revolutions*, Cambridge: Cambridge University Press, 1979. For an analysis applied to the 1989 Tiananmen demonstrations, see Andrew Walder, "The Political Sociology of the Beijing Upheaval of 1989; *Problems of Communism*, 1989, 38: 30–40. See also Dingxin Zhao, "Ecologies of Social Movements: Student Mobilization during the 1989 Prodemocracy Movement in Beijing," *American Journal of Sociology*, 1998, 103: 1493–1529.

9. Ethnic tensions in Tibet and Xinjiang, however, could under some circumstances escalate into a serious movement in favor of secession in these regions. If China's leaders were unable to successfully quell such a challenge and lost control of either of these provinces, that loss might precipitate serious challenges to the leaders from their colleagues on nationalistic grounds. In other words, it is possible that ethnic secession threats, while not generally endemic in China and not inherently a threat to the rest of the system even in the cases of Tibet and Xinjiang, could if successful produce the potential for a more thoroughgoing threat to the regime.

10. By the same general reasoning, it is not clear that rising inequalities in China generally will provide a major impetus for social discontent and political challenges (a specter raised in the recent, controversial book by He Qinglian, *The Pitfalls of China's Modernization*). Although we lack systematic research on Chinese popular beliefs about inequality and distributive justice issues, it seems likely that as in other societies, it is not so much the size of inequalities but perceptions of the predominance of illegitimate and corrupt means of getting ahead that generate most popular anger. And such anger is likely to be focused on specific groups that are seen as unfairly benefiting or causing such unfair benefits, rather than at inequalities in general.

11. On the size of the rural-urban income gap, see my article, "City versus Countryside in China's Development, *Problems of Post-Communism*, 1996, 43:9–22; see also Azizur Khan and Carl Riskin, "Income and Inequality in China: Composition, Distribution, and Growth of Household Income, 1988 to 1995," *China Quarterly*, 1998, 154: 221–53.

12. The best-known example is the popular protests in Renshou County in Sichuan Province in 1993. See the discussion in Miles, *The Legacy of Tiananmen*, pp. 169–73; see also Thomas Bernstein's essay in this volume.

13. In some cases, such as in the Renshou demonstrations, several townships within one county have mobilized together, and in others demonstrations have erupted in several nearby counties over the course of several weeks. See the discussion in

Thomas Bernstein's essay in this volume. However, peasant mobilizations into a movement spanning several counties seems to have been avoided so far.

14. See Lianjiang Li and Kevin O'Brien, "Villagers and Popular Resistance in Contemporary China," *Modern China*, 1996, 22: 28–61.

15. Hao Hongsheng, personal communication to the author, June 1999, concerning a Beijing floating population census conducted in 1997.

16. See the works on China's migrants by Dorothy Solinger, particularly her recent book, *Contesting Citizenship in Urban China*, Berkeley: University of California Press, 1999.

17. See also the discussion in Dorothy Solinger, "China's Transients and the State: A Form of Civil Society? Hong Kong: Institute of Asian-Pacific Studies, Chinese University of Hong Kong, 1991.

18. See my essay, "The Changing Role of Workers," in Merle Goldman and Roderick MacFarquhar, eds., *The Paradox of China's Post-Mao Reforms*, Cambridge: Harvard University Press, 1999. On the stricter labor regime, see the discussion in Minghua Zhao and Theo Nichols, "Management Control of Labour in State-Owned Enterprises: Cases from the Textile Industry," *China Journal*, 1996, 36: 1–24; Wenfang Tang and William Parish, *Chinese Urban Life Under Reform: The Changing Social Contract*, Cambridge: Cambridge University Press, forthcoming, Chapter 6.

19. Many of the most angry worker protests have been outside of the SOE sector, particularly in the sweatshop enterprises financed by Overseas Chinese, Taiwanese, and Korean capital. In such cases abuses of workers, avoidable industrial accidents, and other causes of protests understandably are directed at what are perceived to be their source, local managers and owners, rather than the central state.

20. This conclusion is similar to that reached by Dorothy Solinger in her essay in this volume.

21. See the discussion in Jeffrey Wasserstrom, *Student Protests in Twentieth Century China*, Stanford: Stanford University Press, 1991; and in his essay, "Student Protests and the Chinese Tradition, 1919–1989," in Tony Saich, ed., *The Chinese People's Movement*, Armonk, NY: M.E. Sharpe, 1990.

22. See the evidence presented in Tang and Parish, chapters 3–4.

23. *Falun Gong* is only one of the many examples of sects and would-be messiahs that have arisen in China during the reform period, although it may well be the largest. For another example, a messianic sect based in Hunan Province that claimed more than 10,000 followers in 1997, see Seth Faison, "Strategy for a Charlatan in China: Claim Deity, Then Steal and Seduce," *New York Times*, Sept. 18, 1999, p. A5.

24. For a discussion of the revival of *Qigong* masters and followers in urban China since the 1980s, see Nancy Chen, "Urban Spaces and Experiences of *Qigong*," in D. Davis, R. Kraus, B. Naughton, and E. Perry, eds., *Urban Spaces in Contemporary China*, Cambridge: Cambridge University Press, 1995.

25. The latter term is used in Steven Jackson in the "Conference Summary" of this volume.

26. It is worth noting that the unwillingness or inability of the new generations of East European leaders to resort to large scale coercion to put down growing protests in 1989 was a key factor in the collapse of their regimes. (When the one old generation leader involved, Ceausescu, proved willing, the troops wouldn't obey.)

Contributors

David Shambaugh is Professor of Political Science and International Affairs and Director of the China Policy Program in the Elliott School of International Affairs at George Washington University. He is also a non-resident Senior Fellow in the Foreign Policy Studies Program at The Brookings Institution in Washington, D.C. He is former Editor of *The China Quarterly* and has published widely on various aspects of contemporary Chinese and Asian affairs. His *Reforming China's Military* and edited *The Modern Chinese State* will be published in the year 2000. He recently co-edited *China's Military Faces the Future* (1999) with James Lilley, and *The China Reader: The Reform Era* (1999) with Orville Schell.

Thomas Bernstein is Professor of Political Science at Columbia University. He has published extensively on various aspects of Chinese politics, while his current research relates to the politics of China's rural areas and public sphere. He has recently published chapters in Merle Goldman and Roderick MacFarquhar (eds.), *The Paradox of China's Post-Mao Reforms* and James Morley (ed.), *Driven by Growth: Political Change in the Asia-Pacific Region* (second edition).

Pieter Bottelier recently retired as a country director and senior economist with the World Bank. His long experience in the World Bank includes service in Africa, Latin America, and Asia. He was Chief of the World Bank's resident mission in China from 1993–1997. He is an adjunct professor at Johns Hopkins University Nitze School of Advanced International Studies, and is an independent consultant on economic transition policies and investment.

Bruce Dickson is Associate Professor of Political Science and International Affairs and Director of the Sigur Center of Asian Studies at George Washington University. He is the author of *Democratization in China and Taiwan: The Adaptability of Leninist Parties* (1997), and has published articles in *The China Quarterly, Asian Survey, The National Interest,* and other journals. He is currently writing a book concerned with economic and political reform in China.

June Teufel Dreyer is Professor of Politics at the University of Miami. She has published widely on various aspects of contemporary China and specializes in ethnic minorities and the Chinese military. Her textbook, *China's Political System: Modernization and Tradition,* was recently reprinted by Addison Wesley Longman in its third edition. She is currently writing a book on military relations across the Taiwan Strait.

Merle Goldman is Professor of Chinese History at Boston University, as well as a Research Associate at the Fairbank Center for East Asian Research at Harvard University. She has published numerous studies on the Chinese intelligentsia and other aspects of contemporary Chinese politics, literature, and thought. Her most recent books are *Sowing the Seeds of Democracy in China* (1994), and an expanded edition, co-authored with the late John King Fairbank, of *China: A New History* (1998).

Steven F. Jackson is Associate Professor and Chair of the Department of Political Science at Indiana University of Pennsylvania. He has published articles and book chapters on Chinese foreign policy, Chinese industrial policy, and the Chinese steel industry.

Nicholas Lardy is Senior Fellow in the Foreign Policy Studies Program at The Brookings Institution in Washington, D.C. He previously taught at the University of Washington, where he also served as Director of the Jackson School of International Studies. He has published numerous books and shorter studies on the Chinese economy and foreign trade. His most recent book is entitled *China's Unfinished Economic Revolution* (1998), and he is presently working on a study of China's accession to the World Trade Organization.

H. Lyman Miller is a Visiting Fellow at the Hoover Institution of War, Revolution, and Peace at Stanford University, as well as an Associate

Professor of Chinese Studies at the Naval Postgraduate School in Monterey, California. He previously worked as an analyst at the Foreign Broadcast Information Service and taught for many years at Johns Hopkins University Nitze School of Advanced International Studies in Washington, D.C. An historian by training, he has published widely on various aspects of contemporary Chinese politics and thought. His most recent book is entitled *Science and Dissent in Post-Mao China: The Politics of Knowledge* (1996).

Dorothy Solinger is Professor of Politics and Society at the University of California, Irvine. She has published widely on various aspects of contemporary Chinese politics, political economy, political demography, and comparative politics. Her most recent books are *Contesting Citizenship in Urban China: Peasant Migrants, the State, and the Logic of the Market* (1999), and *China's Transition from Socialism* (1993). Her current research involves China's laid-off workers.

Martin King Whyte is Professor and Chairman of the Sociology Department at George Washington University. A leading specialist on contemporary Chinese social development, he has also published extensively on comparative communist social policy, comparative educational policy, and comparative sociology of the family. His books include (with William Parish): *Village and Family in Contemporary China, Urban Life in Contemporary China,* and *Small Groups and Political Rituals in China.*

Index